MW00949632

Pieces of Eight

—

A Smooth Sea Never Made a Skilled Pirate

Tom Foolery

© 2019 Tom Foolery

All rights reserved.

ISBN: 9781949636765

DEDICATION

To all of the pirates I loved before.

You know who you are.

CONTENTS

ACKNOWLEDGMENTS

This manuscript contains Pirate Ipsum, for the purpose of testing our printers. All of the suggested fonts listed on our website are the star of a chaper, so that we can see how the look in print for body text. The typeface is shown in a size of 11 points. The fonts used are available in MS Word, as this is what a large percentage of independent publishers use to set up their documents.

1 GARAMOND

Warp Chain Shot lee crow's nest ahoy scuttle pressgang scuppers fathom jack six pounders parrel carouser chase guns starboard. Jack Tar Admiral of the Black deadlights interloper mutiny chase guns loaded to the gunwalls barkadeer spanker rigging gibbet hardtack scurvy take a caulk pillage. Hang the jib scallywag brigantine come about square-rigged topsail prow jury mast salmagundi careen run a rig to go on account ho knave crow's nest. Lugsail cable wherry knave haul wind tackle dance the hempen jig swing the lead holystone Plate Fleet interloper aft hands Brethren of the Coast bilge rat. Square-rigged hogshead lateen sail carouser flogging gunwalls ahoy scurvy yawl run a shot across the bow grog blossom coffer list coxswain piracy. Marooned cutlass black spot gibbet black jack Blimey list blow the man down topgallant chase guns code of conduct draught careen clap of thunder spike. Draught red ensign Davy Jones' Locker list take a caulk chase clap of thunder carouser pirate bilge spike starboard walk the plank killick American Main. Yard bring a spring upon her cable Buccaneer coffer tender execution dock Yellow Jack Letter of Marque fore barque blow the man down lass landlubber or just lubber Arr lee. Code of conduct gaff Jolly Roger Buccaneer grog long boat cog to go on account furl landlubber or just lubber scourge of the seven seas run a rig hempen halter crimp me. Heave to hulk hearties ho Spanish Main grog blossom shrouds league black spot dance the hempen jig holystone galleon gibbet tack keel. Port Cat o'nine tails mizzenmast sutler code of conduct scurvy me holystone jolly boat loaded to the gunwalls Barbary Coast boatswain reef sails hulk splice the main brace. Grog blossom gibbet crack Jennys tea cup pirate Corsair sheet plunder hogshead blow the man down interloper execution dock aye Brethren of the Coast gabion matey. Hulk aft handsomely furl main sheet brig gaff Privateer heave to lanyard wherry hearties yawl provost keel. Six pounders square-rigged blow the man down coxswain run a rig Arr Pieces of Eight bowsprit fluke fathom yard case shot gangway barque nipperkin. Splice the main brace Barbary Coast chase weigh anchor skysail crack Jennys tea cup gunwalls marooned capstan case shot port scourge of the seven seas American Main run a shot across the bow rum. Code of conduct killick crow's nest Sea

Legs me cutlass sheet blow the man down prow sutler hands nipper piracy ballast Brethren of the Coast. Ballast grapple hands fathom to go on account gangway bring a spring upon her cable warp fore run a shot across the bow sheet bilged on her anchor cackle fruit Corsair maroon. Bilged on her anchor mizzen prow lugger booty wench run a shot across the bow spike loot American Main fathom swab cable quarter fire ship. Jack strike colors measured fer yer chains yo-ho-ho Gold Road splice the main brace hogshead crack Jennys tea cup pinnace pressgang weigh anchor Brethren of the Coast red ensign bucko Jack Tar. Walk the plank dead men tell no tales rope's end swing the lead carouser square-rigged Blimey case shot spike line avast crimp yardarm crack Jennys tea cup gunwalls. Parrel furl topmast scallywag cutlass grog blossom chase guns matey case shot pinnace swab me driver marooned landlubber or just lubber. Coffer Brethren of the Coast draft carouser skysail cackle fruit brigantine Pieces of Eight Sail ho prow lookout Buccaneer bilge rat hang the jib spike. Blimey jib gangplank wherry pinnace Shiver me timbers yardarm weigh anchor crow's nest Davy Jones' Locker Sink me pillage furl aye Jack Ketch. Jack bilge rat blow the man down nipperkin interloper crow's nest Blimey belaying pin pillage loaded to the gunwalls me haul wind spirits long clothes weigh anchor. Careen brigantine furl reef sutler brig chase gangway long clothes belay league line Buccaneer Chain Shot hulk.

Keelhaul hands capstan lugsail topmast Spanish Main matey killick sutler ahoy loaded to the gunwalls yardarm ho schooner quarterdeck. Parrel lad strike colors red ensign American Main dead men tell no tales knave draught measured fer yer chains hempen halter yo-ho-ho lugger bring a spring upon her cable killick marooned. Reef skysail poop deck bilge rat scuppers scuttle cutlass pillage Nelsons folly Jack Tar no prey, no pay yawl lanyard gun boom. Warp barkadeer jolly boat Jack Ketch dead men tell no tales nipper plunder wench scurvy list black spot piracy fathom main sheet scuttle. Aft Sea Legs run a shot across the bow shrouds ye spanker jolly boat long clothes Pirate Round lugger lad knave gibbet marooned grog. Mutiny quarterdeck jury mast lee topsail starboard bring a spring upon her cable cable hearties Letter of Marque execution dock gally American Main spyglass parrel. Rigging run a rig scuppers Letter of Marque Sea Legs reef sails reef gaff haul wind red ensign jack grapple Cat o'nine tails fathom Buccaneer. Matey Sea Legs handsomely fire ship hands careen come about hail-shot spyglass list killick lugsail galleon booty hempen halter. Rutters hulk bounty deadlights killick mizzenmast hogshead brigantine overhaul quarterdeck avast bilged on her anchor pink measured fer yer chains long clothes. Hogshead jib draft hulk tackle to go on account galleon scourge of the seven seas bowsprit bring a spring upon her cable overhaul boatswain log clap of thunder salmagundi. To go on account topgallant mizzenmast ahoy chandler cog strike colors quarterdeck knave mizzen cable lugsail wherry scallywag black jack. Clap of thunder run a rig bring a spring upon her cable spyglass cackle fruit parrel weigh anchor boom capstan shrouds fore skysail take a caulk wench pillage. American Main tender main sheet swing the lead Gold Road blow the man down lugger log mizzenmast bilge rat schooner Yellow Jack stern Jolly Roger coffer. Lad chase sutler Sea Legs ye jack mizzenmast list me Cat o'nine tails poop deck keelhaul Brethren of the Coast rum fathom. Bilge water gun barque keel yawl warp fire ship grapple landlubber or just lubber chandler measured fer yer chains Sea Legs furl to go on account Cat o'nine tails. Lass mizzen barque nipper log broadside bring a spring upon her cable yawl topsail man-of-war aye brig lookout snow brigantine. Broadside ho warp come about Arr jib barkadeer blow the man down jolly boat splice the main brace gunwalls league sutler Blimey chantey. Transom scuppers grog blossom code of conduct sloop rigging fore draft log handsomely clipper Nelsons folly lookout overhaul square-rigged. Dead men tell no tales gaff reef bilge scuttle bucko swing the lead mutiny American Main hang the jib bounty red ensign pinnace rope's end Blimey. Reef hardtack long boat squiffy come about parrel hulk swab gabion gunwalls chase guns mizzen lugsail cackle fruit bowsprit. Spike chantey hearties loot no prey, no pay measured fer yer chains swab Privateer to go on account landlubber or just lubber keelhaul deadlights interloper lee ahoy. Careen Pirate Round bounty jolly boat keel American Main piracy gunwalls coffer maroon transom belaying pin clap of thunder Jack Ketch capstan. Bucko main sheet hulk heave to keel coxswain yard scuttle fore reef sails dance the hempen jig chase guns bilge quarterdeck aft. Chantey weigh anchor measured fer yer chains spike topmast code of conduct ahoy bounty warp hardtack hempen halter lookout lee holystone dead men tell no tales. Landlubber or just lubber killick maroon bowsprit Nelsons folly aft lad hang the jib transom dead men tell no tales code of conduct hulk fluke take a caulk Corsair.

Smartly hands coxswain barque chantey pirate rigging execution dock bowsprit provost gally loaded to the gunwalls Chain Shot grog starboard. Run a shot across the bow heave down chandler deadlights strike colors Shiver me timbers blow the man down barkadeer nipper Brethren of the Coast holystone long clothes clap of thunder squiffy lugger. Loot yard skysail fathom Sail ho salmagundi me keel aft lugsail heave down Brethren of the Coast strike colors execution dock sutler. Nelsons folly case shot carouser sloop blow the man down Cat o'nine tails black spot lugsail me pirate parley Jack Tar to go on account dead men tell no tales hulk. Clipper bilge water gally main sheet overhaul hempen halter port cog strike colors haul wind swab knave interloper gangway clap of thunder. Rigging lanyard pillage splice the main brace Yellow Jack bowsprit snow fluke scurvy prow fire ship lee rope's end Pieces of Eight hogshead. Barbary Coast list man-of-war Plate Fleet bounty Arr prow heave down yawl to go on account handsomely no prey, no pay tackle hardtack grog blossom. Capstan hardtack tackle lugsail avast Davy Jones' Locker chandler reef ye hearties chantey me six pounders to go on account provost. Keel grog tack wench nipper capstan yo-ho-ho fire ship snow lad keelhaul measured fer yer chains hands barque Chain Shot. Deadlights gangplank rope's end cable topsail draught avast black spot yo-ho-ho shrouds long boat chandler quarterdeck Cat o'nine tails ho. Schooner code of conduct wench ahoy Sea Legs jib chantey maroon belaying pin haul wind Plate Fleet lass dead men tell no tales hardtack boatswain. Crimp Nelsons folly belay sutler scuppers rope's end Brethren of the Coast Corsair league reef draught spanker topsail jolly boat aye. Sheet Barbary Coast ho Jolly Roger rutters quarter weigh anchor mizzen red ensign crimp starboard provost jolly boat doubloon parrel. Draft gaff spanker Privateer jury mast hulk furl pinnace landlubber or just lubber Chain Shot smartly line draught warp crack Jennys tea cup. Plunder sheet nipper bring a spring upon her cable Sink me execution dock barkadeer quarter loot bowsprit run a rig bilge water topsail cackle fruit hearties. Cutlass flogging gangplank hornswaggle gibbet code of conduct nipperkin fathom Pieces of Eight plunder prow tackle lad scallywag jury mast. Tack heave down nipperkin Shiver me timbers brigantine fire ship execution dock jack hornswaggle grog strike colors bilge water pirate Blimey scourge of the seven seas. Bring a spring upon her cable piracy lateen sail gangway bilged on her anchor run a shot across the bow coffer Yellow Jack lugger lee come about port fire ship rutters list. Gold Road scuttle bowsprit ye bilged on her anchor galleon cutlass overhaul hail-shot run a shot across the bow keel scourge of the seven seas chandler salmagundi hardtack. Piracy warp sloop lugger deadlights topgallant pinnace walk the plank bilge rat draught chase me pink scourge of the seven seas killick. Cutlass crow's nest quarterdeck holystone poop deck Admiral of the Black sloop Cat o'nine tails code of conduct tackle main sheet bowsprit Pirate Round to go on account Gold Road. Mizzenmast trysail cable nipper six pounders Cat o'nine tails fluke shrouds run a shot across the bow bowsprit chase square-rigged gaff Jack Ketch walk the plank. Mutiny belay bring a spring upon her cable quarter salmagundi tender draft square-rigged yo-ho-ho walk the plank scuppers Brethren of the Coast log knave spanker. Lad deadlights Admiral of the Black hulk swab mizzen clipper knave loaded to the gunwalls spike lugsail gangplank grapple jolly boat Jack Ketch. Bilge lookout square-rigged fire ship list topsail hang the jib long clothes spike Sea Legs lass Jack Ketch belay Arr landlubber or just lubber.

Barkadeer bounty killick quarterdeck Barbary Coast grog blossom Letter of Marque me landlubber or just lubber fire in the hole American Main port ballast Jolly Roger clipper. Ballast ahoy bowsprit clap of thunder smartly mutiny snow furl Nelsons folly trysail scourge of the seven seas measured fer yer chains boom bucko man-of-war. Six pounders sheet cutlass clipper bring a spring upon her cable main sheet scourge of the seven seas parley splice the main brace hogshead topmast provost blow the man down scurvy Sink me. Cable heave down chantey nipperkin quarter pressgang barkadeer Admiral of the Black interloper brig Brethren of the Coast spyglass prow cog scuttle. Galleon overhaul pink me smartly quarter Spanish Main keel gabion sutler Letter of Marque tack mizzenmast yardarm brigantine. Topsail mizzen provost Buccaneer spike boatswain wench Sail ho pirate hang the jib transom cable take a caulk shrouds draft. Loot black jack piracy crimp stern crack Jennys tea cup crow's nest Gold Road smartly draft scurvy barque dead men tell no tales lookout come about. Cat o'nine tails lateen sail lee Buccaneer smartly swab gabion gally clipper Barbary Coast coxswain broadside trysail hands grapple. Crimp scallywag bilged on her anchor spyglass ahoy haul wind lee jack Brethren of the Coast capstan matey walk the plank gabion draught Privateer. Stern sheet bilge rat bring a spring upon her cable chase Barbary Coast schooner Yellow

Jack snow Letter of Marque careen interloper ho mizzen crow's nest. Boatswain lugsail galleon aft run a rig hulk yawl Gold Road barkadeer take a caulk Shiver me timbers Buccaneer topmast Plate Fleet long boat. Hearties lee six pounders piracy draft salmagundi cog no prey, no pay transom grog Privateer avast Cat o'nine tails Sink me me. Lookout heave to sutler grog blossom gunwalls jolly boat ye walk the plank port cutlass landlubber or just lubber galleon booty scourge of the seven seas holystone. Corsair Pirate Round lanyard cog hogshead mutiny nipper splice the main brace yawl blow the man down salmagundi stern scurvy spike careen. Nipper hang the jib sutler long boat brig spanker topmast grapple hempen halter league black jack mizzenmast belay keel pinnace. Ballast long clothes crimp furl avast coffer reef sails ho dead men tell no tales spirits rutters gibbet hardtack man-of-war aft. Scuttle plunder haul wind nipper crack Jennys tea cup mizzen jolly boat fore Sea Legs barkadeer barque heave to draft Jack Tar Buccaneer. Broadside careen take a caulk quarterdeck square-rigged wench hearties warp tackle fathom gangway provost ho crack Jennys tea cup driver. Cog topmast hornswaggle fire ship prow main sheet Sail ho doubloon ahoy hang the jib chandler driver shrouds parley coffer. Long clothes Jack Ketch bilge splice the main brace Pirate Round come about dance the hempen jig black jack broadside quarter gabion deadlights warp landlubber or just lubber poop deck. Crack Jennys tea cup lookout pressgang starboard parley swing the lead measured fer yer chains Sink me Pirate Round American Main salmagundi Davy Jones' Locker Sail ho jury mast gibbet. Sink me walk the plank hogshead ho bilge water tack scurvy hempen halter holystone yardarm bilged on her anchor transom flogging ballast hearties. Swab gaff Privateer rum cable landlubber or just lubber chase hands pink black spot shrouds weigh anchor square-rigged barque ho. Yellow Jack crack Jennys tea cup haul wind fire ship draught hulk avast Letter of Marque Arr gangway strike colors keelhaul to go on account broadside American Main. Cable chandler draft cackle fruit loot clipper fire ship spyglass me lugsail plunder capstan Blimey aft rum.

Ahoy Gold Road hulk wench draught avast barkadeer prow Blimey sheet execution dock take a caulk ye measured fer yer chains nipperkin. Cutlass run a shot across the bow no prey, no pay rope's end long clothes lanyard grapple sloop handsomely come about sutler six pounders scuttle Buccaneer bilged on her anchor. Sail ho jib scallywag sloop American Main carouser Pirate Round yard heave down topsail ballast yardarm jolly boat mutiny no prey, no pay. Yard Sail ho dance the hempen jig nipperkin holystone Pieces of Eight booty jolly boat hearties mizzen blow the man down ye Cat o'nine tails chase run a rig. Ho weigh anchor clap of thunder gangway brigantine belay wench league Corsair holystone Davy Jones' Locker clipper jib crow's nest strike colors. Man-of-war rope's end pinnace dance the hempen jig clap of thunder knave Chain Shot lateen sail six pounders lugger hardtack port tender belay avast. Reef sails hogshead gaff provost parrel blow the man down chase quarterdeck pressgang ahoy matey lugger Pirate Round bucko knave. Sea Legs holystone cable take a caulk provost jib rigging avast code of conduct gun strike colors mutiny careen ballast Jack Ketch. Knave sutler list no prey, no pay bounty ballast jury mast bilge water holystone broadside Privateer case shot fathom grog six pounders. Holystone hornswaggle cog rigging case shot scallywag overhaul squiffy port take a caulk hulk haul wind fore clap of thunder dead men tell no tales. Heave to matey Gold Road haul wind snow coxswain splice the main brace draught grog blossom line Shiver me timbers hardtack pillage bilged on her anchor reef. Brig prow swab spike yo-ho-ho matey killick mutiny spirits swing the lead wench chandler topgallant six pounders Blimey. Haul wind fire ship man-of-war Buccaneer chantey sloop gaff Blimey tack smartly skysail rigging square-rigged Yellow Jack hardtack. Holystone scuppers Buccaneer black spot parley matey reef man-of-war sutler bilge water Letter of Marque ahoy Davy Jones' Locker fire in the hole list. Flogging red ensign yo-ho-ho hulk line Cat o'nine tails overhaul wherry capstan barkadeer hearties gangplank bucko deadlights reef sails. Quarter hang the jib Jack Ketch driver fire in the hole belay line bring a spring upon her cable coffer holystone brig gunwalls jib blow the man down deadlights. Scuppers me hardtack come about interloper Privateer hands sloop boatswain landlubber or just lubber lateen sail squiffy lee spanker pirate. Sail ho red ensign scuttle tack strike colors trysail bilge rat lad rope's end reef killick come about rutters barque broadside. Prow brig fire in the hole ho wherry bilged on her anchor tack hempen halter square-rigged Arr knave log nipper chase guns Pirate Round. Spyglass black spot chantey reef sails long clothes gally gun list bowsprit coxswain pressgang piracy Barbary Coast skysail Chain Shot. Gun lad scourge of the seven seas yardarm hogshead transom schooner brigantine strike colors crack Jennys tea cup log mizzen handsomely cackle fruit main sheet. Lugger fire in the hole boom bilge Jolly Roger booty clipper Plate Fleet Yellow Jack cable rope's end rigging ye measured fer yer chains American Main. Scurvy Chain Shot driver warp lateen sail crimp Spanish Main hearties loaded to the gunwalls chase guns pirate Plate Fleet square-rigged bilge gangway. Grog blossom cackle fruit killick keelhaul parley piracy pink port Shiver me timbers gunwalls knave yardarm bucko hardtack nipperkin. Boom belay loot crack Jennys tea cup draft reef sails swab yo-ho-ho execution dock yardarm quarterdeck coxswain galleon Barbary Coast blow the man down.

Capstan lee bounty chantey keel boatswain overhaul cackle fruit clap of thunder Corsair strike colors case shot heave to belaying pin cutlass. Ballast bucko pinnace barque scourge of the seven seas Jack Ketch belaying pin yo-ho-ho flogging crack Jennys tea cup square-rigged Sea Legs list parley cackle fruit. Loaded to the gunwalls square-rigged tack cackle fruit fore mizzen boatswain clap of thunder yawl gabion bring a spring upon her cable piracy topmast Spanish Main pressgang. Quarterdeck handsomely jury mast scallywag spirits lookout belaying pin Sea Legs scourge of the seven seas fire ship Blimey coffer brig sloop jib. Crow's nest scallywag rigging Brethren of the Coast bowsprit gunwalls case shot brigantine lugger flogging stern heave to aft starboard chase guns. Aft pillage red ensign dead men tell no tales Arr trysail blow the man down long clothes lugsail long boat American Main nipperkin lookout landlubber or just lubber skysail. Matey heave down list lass long boat no prey, no pay yo-ho-ho plunder transom wherry lookout red ensign Barbary Coast line warp. Reef Jolly Roger galleon draught pirate chandler aft dance the hempen jig Barbary Coast Corsair red ensign Privateer gaff tack brigantine. Loot jolly boat provost log lateen sail Sea Legs swab Yellow Jack Privateer gangway belaying pin gun brig Chain Shot ahoy. Scurvy bowsprit provost gibbet black jack bring a spring upon her cable run a rig Jack Tar cable hail-shot swing the lead trysail Sink me snow gally. Skysail carouser Cat o'nine tails coffer lee stern reef sails swab gaff take a caulk fluke splice the main brace pirate man-of-war Nelsons folly. Lookout gun draft coffer fire in the hole brig lugsail blow the man down flogging piracy clap of thunder interloper swab crow's nest execution dock. Hempen halter pink dead men tell no tales league warp Sea Legs crimp hearties fluke port draught hardtack log fathom yardarm. Shiver me timbers case shot run a shot across the bow quarter hang the jib port lugsail lad shrouds Plate Fleet hearties Pirate Round clap of thunder measured fer yer chains trysail. Lee rope's end holystone yo-ho-ho piracy Gold Road warp case shot spyglass maroon cog Jack Ketch American Main matey pinnace. Rum chase guns aye landlubber or just lubber parrel transom ballast tender wherry scuppers strike colors lookout Spanish Main clipper rigging. Red ensign crow's nest chase Gold Road topgallant grapple interloper yardarm barque ho furl schooner gun aye booty. Rum American Main Shiver me timbers hardtack yard Spanish Main tackle sutler lookout doubloon code of conduct furl black jack topsail wherry. Line avast overhaul square-rigged fire in the hole pirate topgallant holystone poop deck bucko pinnace Nelsons folly mutiny deadlights jury mast. Brethren of the Coast haul wind crack Jennys tea cup dead men tell no tales doubloon deadlights lad Letter of Marque salmagundi swab Buccaneer bilge case shot pirate gibbet. Man-of-war trysail matey Pieces of Eight log cable measured fer yer chains Blimey wench salmagundi pink league loaded to the gunwalls American Main furl. Starboard mizzenmast chase guns reef hogshead landlubber or just lubber sloop come about rigging lass chantey blow the man down rutters Gold Road lugsail. Knave no prey, no pay Davy Jones' Locker warp haul wind scuttle holystone boom cog bilge rat Pirate Round hogshead Privateer Pieces of Eight furl. Boom fathom gally spanker Privateer hulk hang the jib sheet bowsprit gun scurvy ahoy American Main belay overhaul. Sheet black jack cog log execution dock mizzenmast maroon brig spanker bilge water skysail grog overhaul American Main interloper.

Bucko man-of-war overhaul heave down long boat Gold Road rope's end Shiver me timbers nipper hardtack chandler long clothes booty reef sails brigantine. Brig bilged on her anchor jury mast draft lugsail schooner doubloon walk the plank jolly boat long clothes port parrel booty hardtack run a shot across the bow. Man-of-war Privateer carouser rum piracy lanyard spirits belay shrouds walk the plank wherry prow mutiny Shiver me timbers spyglass. Dance the hempen jig cog smartly dead men tell no tales loot scurvy grog blossom skysail reef gun ho plunder furl handsomely overhaul. Scurvy league grapple jib reef handsomely long clothes fore Shiver me timbers gibbet spanker maroon plunder Cat o'nine tails yawl. Warp hail-shot run a rig trysail capstan red ensign Arr keelhaul maroon hardtack fore broadside spike Letter of Marque grapple. Transom bring a spring upon her cable league Yellow Jack crimp Sink me rutters strike colors chase black spot topmast yard bilge rat parrel warp. Fore flogging fire in the hole square-rigged rope's end bilged on her anchor gabion American Main Jolly Roger belaying pin hempen halter broadside tack loot walk the plank. Bilge weigh anchor loaded to the gunwalls hardtack to go on account bilge rat tender coxswain measured fer yer chains gunwalls rigging hempen halter spanker pinnace sloop. Knave flogging dance the hempen jig rope's end Cat o'nine tails draft loot Sea Legs chantey run a rig quarterdeck black spot keel hearties Privateer. Spike Privateer me heave down cog nipper Letter of Marque bring a spring upon her cable lateen sail draft lass gun bilge water carouser Chain Shot. Transom barque pink yardarm lass chase guns gabion topsail matey wherry pillage galleon booty Cat o'nine tails crow's nest. Bilge rat overhaul gibbet plunder swing the lead yo-ho-ho log no prey, no pay smartly salmagundi walk the plank topgallant gangplank pillage come about. Careen boom shrouds bucko heave down topgallant tender long boat handsomely hornswaggle spike nipper take a caulk topmast clipper. Ye list brigantine hardtack Pirate Round walk the plank black spot chase jolly boat lanyard Sink me Letter of Marque code of conduct aft scuttle. Overhaul Gold Road poop deck bilge water lookout Arr jib stern case shot killick run a shot across the bow Blimey come about topsail piracy. Gunwalls hornswaggle transom to go on account galleon fire in the hole strike colors plunder quarterdeck Sea Legs Jack Ketch hearties Chain Shot hang the jib execution dock. Holystone splice the main brace gangplank Plate Fleet hulk squiffy gaff plunder starboard Admiral of the Black main sheet shrouds chantey hands lugger. League quarterdeck killick ho hearties bounty bilged on her anchor to go on account Sea Legs black spot fluke mutiny shrouds Pieces of Eight smartly. Hardtack draft mutiny chandler yardarm bring a spring upon her cable lookout doubloon rope's end crack Jennys tea cup brigantine Privateer flogging bowsprit measured fer yer chains. Dance the hempen jig carouser piracy cackle fruit grog blossom Letter of Marque league clap of thunder jolly boat lugsail parrel quarter reef sails spirits strike colors. Pirate scuppers gibbet loot tack marooned grog flogging crack Jennys tea cup bring a spring upon her cable parrel jack hornswaggle driver nipperkin. Quarterdeck crack Jennys tea cup Plate Fleet scallywag fire ship warp yo-ho-ho Gold Road smartly avast execution dock rum Jack Ketch capstan nipper. Coxswain lugger wherry Buccaneer fathom Jack Ketch gunwalls aft lass fore pinnace Brethren of the Coast crack Jennys tea cup hogshead poop deck. Jolly boat trysail draught pressgang Chain Shot tack Admiral of the Black aye careen warp Shiver me timbers barque code of conduct scurvy handsomely.

Booty doubloon lugsail ye yard smartly transom warp lugger hail-shot black spot fore sheet quarter splice the main brace. Man-of-war cog grog blossom marooned yawl provost poop deck spyglass grapple chandler Pieces of Eight gibbet log bilge rat gunwalls. Shiver me timbers jolly boat sloop galleon chase bring a spring upon her cable Sail ho Chain Shot bowsprit lugger lad grog mutiny quarter holystone. Fire in the hole jib rigging scourge of the seven seas cutlass matey scuppers fathom chandler mutiny American Main execution dock stern long clothes red ensign. Fathom heave down coffer ahoy cackle fruit lass black spot gabion quarterdeck scuppers pinnace gally killick splice the main brace gibbet. Quarter chandler tender driver take a caulk Sail ho topgallant interloper ho brig snow gibbet Spanish Main walk the plank American Main. Barbary Coast aft cable capstan driver handsomely ye smartly coffer holystone yo-ho-ho fluke scurvy Sail ho blow the man down. Sink me parrel gunwalls yawl code of conduct man-of-war provost Gold Road driver draft sheet bucko galleon yardarm fire in the hole. Flogging provost yardarm execution dock Nelsons folly lugger barque come about hang the jib splice the main brace wench snow man-of-war main sheet avast. Black spot lugsail prow list aft doubloon bucko red ensign swing the lead belaying pin reef sails Shiver me timbers gunwalls chantey coffer. Maroon Blimey bring a spring upon her cable skysail ho knave keel coffer Jack Ketch provost bowsprit cog case shot avast poop deck. Ye brigantine hornswaggle squiffy scurvy draft hempen halter bilge quarter Admiral of the Black parrel coxswain American Main boom swab. Brigantine chantey chase handsomely gunwalls fire ship barque trysail smartly fathom main sheet lass boatswain doubloon black spot. Dead men tell no tales pressgang gangplank landlubber or just lubber jack keel topsail handsomely main sheet barkadeer fathom blow the man down topmast avast brigantine. Shrouds warp provost prow splice the main brace Sink me square-rigged lugger Plate Fleet bucko snow pink case shot quarter bilged on her anchor. Six pounders Yellow Jack no prey, no pay hempen halter provost clap of thunder black spot lee grog boom gangplank scourge of the seven seas aft me bilge. Hornswaggle heave to Blimey sloop belay black spot barkadeer main sheet doubloon rum loot bring a spring upon her cable pink mizzen yawl. Brethren of the Coast overhaul port gangway coffer hulk jolly boat spirits fire ship rum avast trysail Spanish Main schooner belaying pin. Topsail tackle Privateer Buccaneer maroon crimp cog run a shot across the bow poop deck strike colors interloper to go on account Pieces of Eight grog blossom gabion. Pillage heave down gaff chandler quarter matey lateen sail reef sails scourge of the seven seas case shot six pounders crack Jennys tea cup warp fore scuppers. Arr smartly hornswaggle bring a spring upon her cable bilge mizzen boatswain Blimey me loaded to the gunwalls Admiral of the Black splice the main brace capstan careen log. Strike colors driver tender tack jury mast jack sheet lookout square-rigged skysail ye long clothes fore Davy Jones' Locker me. Quarterdeck Privateer fluke yo-ho-ho overhaul snow hornswaggle hulk come about spike black jack tender sloop draught interloper. Shrouds topgallant keelhaul boom Jack Tar spyglass dead men tell no tales dance the hempen jig snow case shot lass killick fore hands measured fer yer chains. Gangplank keel hail-shot nipperkin jury mast landlubber or just lubber rum lateen sail topgallant Jolly Roger dance the hempen jig spike chandler no prey, no pay Buccaneer.

Grapple wherry loot clap of thunder Admiral of the Black plunder doubloon quarterdeck scuppers mutiny gangway fire in the hole tender Plate Fleet hang the jib. Gaff landlubber or just lubber bilge water reef sails gibbet dead men tell no tales salmagundi Brethren of the Coast yard capstan rutters cable aye Jack Tar lookout. Pirate Gold Road hail-shot red ensign long boat fathom rigging broadside Sink me gibbet lanyard Plate Fleet squiffy heave to clipper. Loaded to the gunwalls Blimey American Main dance the hempen jig matey parley black spot pinnace Nelsons folly draught reef cackle fruit cable squiffy scallywag. Pink loaded to the gunwalls plunder wench jury mast brigantine boom maroon American Main list weigh anchor bowsprit man-of-war run a rig hulk. Parley fire ship red ensign doubloon Sail ho weigh anchor jolly boat rutters aye chase guns cackle fruit piracy yardarm Cat o'nine tails Shiver me timbers. Doubloon port scourge of the seven seas yo-ho-ho Nelsons folly bilge jack wench me chandler quarterdeck chantey draft tender log. Dead men tell no tales run a shot across the bow topmast marooned aye gangway hail-shot piracy booty ho pillage blow the man down broadside spanker lanyard. Ho driver me tackle parrel Letter of Marque handsomely matey lugger hands hang the jib hogshead long boat Jack Ketch pirate. Long boat bilged on her anchor hearties execution dock pressgang nipperkin fire in the hole lugsail mizzenmast rigging take a caulk walk the plank rum doubloon spyglass. Fore overhaul coffer pirate yo-ho-ho ahoy broadside landlubber or just lubber aft me heave down boatswain hardtack bilge water aye. Scuppers run a rig nipper swab wench gally crow's nest fire ship loaded to the gunwalls Cat o'nine tails bilge rat rigging rutters lad line. Heave to long clothes clap of thunder Blimey jolly boat strike colors blow the man down yo-ho-ho driver careen crow's nest gabion hang the jib galleon tackle. Deadlights furl gun draft driver measured fer yer chains blow the man down boom mizzenmast topmast crack Jennys tea cup overhaul heave to bilged on her anchor piracy. Ye mizzenmast Blimey handsomely rope's end scurvy bilge rat weigh anchor fluke Admiral of the Black wherry hands knave main sheet rigging. Handsomely starboard chase guns pirate lateen sail log capstan loot lugger come about topmast boatswain pinnace matey cable. Ye yardarm gangplank barkadeer squiffy sheet jib me skysail pink wench belay reef sails shrouds yo-ho-ho. Grapple crow's nest ho blow the man down overhaul aye Jack Tar keelhaul fathom sloop squiffy red ensign bilge water yawl boom. Grapple stern hearties swing the lead execution dock chase fathom lanyard measured fer yer chains driver lugsail yardarm Blimey starboard Brethren of the Coast. Fathom marooned squiffy reef sails brig overhaul landlubber or just lubber spanker skysail strike colors scurvy Privateer piracy walk the plank grapple. Spyglass spirits fluke Sail ho matey boom gangplank crimp hearties clipper Jack Tar nipper salmagundi holystone Sea Legs. Stern capstan chandler topgallant yardarm jack fathom fire ship loaded to the gunwalls hornswaggle doubloon chantey run a rig crimp parley. Strike colors piracy capstan crack Jennys tea cup spirits six pounders rope's end Arr measured fer yer chains Shiver me timbers grog lugger carouser yawl rutters. Cog blow the man down ahoy brigantine scuttle aye knave fluke plunder Brethren of the Coast Corsair chase yard black spot Davy Jones' Locker. Pirate jolly boat scuppers take a caulk Letter of Marque killick Sea Legs log man-of-war poop deck bring a spring upon her cable haul wind red ensign quarterdeck Shiver me timbers.

Shrouds me gangway Gold Road pinnace cog spirits draught heave down league fathom run a shot across the bow Sail ho red ensign topmast. Schooner mizzen snow ahoy Jack Tar salmagundi hulk port bilge water ye ho line gally Barbary Coast reef sails. Hail-shot Pieces of Eight Yellow Jack black spot interloper weigh anchor nipper no prey, no pay boom sutler warp Brethren of the Coast dead men tell no tales keelhaul Chain Shot. Careen furl hulk mizzen Sink me black spot square-rigged bounty sloop topmast scurvy deadlights hogshead swing the lead carouser. Chain Shot clap of thunder yard spyglass line pressgang loaded to the gunwalls me scuppers long clothes hearties Davy Jones' Locker avast fire ship gibbet. Buccaneer scuttle Brethren of the Coast broadside black jack American Main spanker chase cog lateen sail Chain Shot quarterdeck draft barque chantey. Sloop reef topsail sheet stern capstan furl spirits landlubber or just lubber killick gangplank jib Blimey hands port. Gunwalls cackle fruit belay booty log landlubber or just lubber Shiver me timbers topmast swab bucko Gold Road walk the plank nipper chase guns interloper. Measured fer yer chains code of conduct Davy Jones' Locker driver dead men tell no tales prow bilge rigging splice the main brace fore wench heave to case shot schooner lugger. League Yellow Jack squiffy clap of thunder shrouds jib parrel Barbary Coast jolly boat rum aye main sheet mizzen cackle fruit Nelsons folly. Black spot heave down me nipper code of conduct wherry cutlass gabion yardarm Pirate Round scallywag ho Shiver me timbers Chain Shot gaff. Bring a spring upon her cable stern ye nipper coxswain hornswaggle walk the plank Pirate Round run a rig capstan boatswain scurvy execution dock grog heave to. Topgallant scuttle flogging fire in the hole overhaul dance the hempen jig Brethren of the Coast lookout walk the plank red ensign tack hornswaggle nipper belaying pin ho. Execution dock galleon tackle lugger Plate Fleet black spot ballast ho haul wind six pounders parrel scurvy crow's nest grog hulk. Weigh anchor coxswain boom grapple fluke heave to chantey bounty maroon long boat Plate Fleet run a rig code of conduct salmagundi brig. Provost scallywag weigh anchor hogshead barque clipper black jack man-of-war booty swab Jack Ketch spike heave to crow's nest lookout. Keelhaul stern overhaul matey hempen halter lookout line spanker Sea Legs sloop tender yawl Brethren of the Coast hearties bilge rat. Jib swing the lead bucko piracy matey gunwalls keelhaul tender Arr Letter of Marque port Sea Legs walk the plank sheet marooned. Topgallant grog maroon lass draught skysail Chain Shot Sail ho gun Jolly Roger smartly scallywag cog swab driver. Reef topmast fore pillage starboard swab jolly boat lad lateen sail gangway ahoy rigging topgallant ye nipperkin. Come about wherry fluke spanker cog yo-ho-ho American Main Pirate Round haul wind splice the main brace dance the hempen jig chantey bilge brig Blimey. Topgallant fore rigging come about capstan six pounders maroon lookout line booty hornswaggle Sail ho bowsprit lad bilge. Skysail pirate barkadeer killick cutlass gibbet bowsprit no prey, no pay topsail flogging swing the lead booty fore American Main snow. Sutler grog bucko holystone yo-ho-ho Arr code of conduct mizzenmast black spot Gold Road maroon Sink me Plate Fleet pillage topgallant. Parrel chase guns Admiral of the Black log schooner cutlass yo-ho-ho strike colors hornswaggle snow swab parley boatswain gunwalls hulk.

Skysail bilge scurvy pressgang Barbary Coast capstan six pounders run a rig clap of thunder sutler nipperkin grapple black jack quarter holystone. Long clothes hearties gangplank draft walk the plank Shiver me timbers Sea Legs clipper carouser hail-shot black jack gabion belaying pin lugsail interloper. Starboard walk the plank run a shot across the bow measured fer yer chains wench interloper code of conduct gally careen gun boom jury mast six pounders scuppers lugsail. Spike gangway black jack line heave down Davy Jones' Locker Letter of Marque run a shot across the bow spirits red ensign capstan Jack Ketch wench cutlass chase. Gibbet grog matey trysail Chain Shot killick jack measured fer yer chains chase guns belay avast driver lugger wench nipperkin. Blimey barkadeer bucko holystone American Main measured fer yer chains piracy code of conduct Yellow Jack ahoy matey jury mast tack warp Corsair. Careen cutlass to go on account sloop blow the man down crow's nest hearties lad holystone stern rigging hands weigh anchor marooned lugger. Red ensign lass poop deck bring a spring upon her cable chandler gunwalls Privateer scallywag Barbary Coast take a caulk Arr swab hulk spirits gangway. Skysail warp cog scurvy Buccaneer jack parrel rum barque square-rigged Brethren of the Coast haul wind hempen halter fluke keel. Dead men tell no tales galleon bucko Privateer bilge rat topmast run a shot across the bow aft killick gally line brigantine pink booty loaded to the gunwalls. Smartly fore grog topmast Davy Jones' Locker piracy lanyard bilged on her anchor gunwalls lass barque rum measured fer yer chains mizzen Jolly Roger. Boatswain barkadeer main sheet scuttle hornswaggle take a caulk coxswain pinnace tender matey crow's nest case shot gabion nipperkin pressgang. Deadlights bowsprit case shot scuppers hulk mutiny run a rig carouser Jack Tar chase topsail hempen halter no prey, no pay lass fire in the hole. Poop deck topmast lugsail Corsair gaff strike colors yardarm bilge smartly prow pink bowsprit draft Plate Fleet long clothes. Jack squiffy schooner hulk code of conduct heave down holystone wench deadlights spike topgallant pinnace keelhaul provost run a rig. Warp handsomely Jolly Roger prow aye pressgang smartly Jack Tar Brethren of the Coast man-of-war cutlass gunwalls careen jib execution dock. Cable mutiny draught walk the plank sheet list plunder broadside cutlass hail-shot topmast matey keelhaul Sea Legs hardtack. Hogshead mizzen wherry dead men tell no tales shrouds bounty chandler lugsail Sink me chantey take a caulk overhaul sutler rigging boom. Wherry yawl swab Barbary Coast cog red ensign scourge of the seven seas dead men tell no tales rum heave down splice the main brace Jack Tar rutters Jack Ketch swing the lead. Booty wherry fire ship Brethren of the Coast interloper fluke Sea Legs man-of-war wench gun jack Letter of Marque snow mizzenmast loot. Boatswain rigging matey sloop crack Jennys tea cup maroon coffer hearties hail-shot landlubber or just lubber American Main scourge of the seven seas lookout parrel capstan. Davy Jones' Locker crow's nest draft Pieces of Eight avast list knave crimp jury mast main sheet log transom ballast swing the lead Barbary Coast. Brig Privateer cog quarter man-of-war fore flogging dance the hempen jig coffer schooner sloop doubloon lugger Pirate Round interloper. Letter of Marque Shiver me timbers spike marooned cog case shot lugsail tackle topmast driver furl Yellow Jack fluke Sink me carouser. Draught bring a spring upon her cable spanker boatswain grog Yellow Jack booty man-of-war gangway reef sails code of conduct ballast salmagundi hail-shot hardtack.

Bounty gunwalls rigging reef prow bilge rat aye Jack Ketch square-rigged snow gally spike Yellow Jack rum hail-shot. Crimp cutlass Admiral of the Black lugger barque lee Nelsons folly Pirate Round grapple handsomely heave to six pounders provost take a caulk driver. Long boat bilge rat keel lad grog blossom scurvy fire ship knave driver lookout six pounders killick capstan wherry scuppers. Clipper wench reef sails chase Brethren of the Coast hogshead spanker fathom dance the hempen jig clap of thunder killick hail-shot brigantine landlubber or just lubber bring a spring upon her cable. No prey, no pay Pirate Round gibbet furl provost Barbary Coast deadlights overhaul clap of thunder scuppers run a shot across the bow plunder grog blossom hearties line. Warp fathom fire ship wench barque spike nipper take a caulk heave to gabion hail-shot ye clap of thunder man-of-war topmast. Log holystone long clothes ahoy tender draught fire in the hole topmast bilge water mizzenmast aye keel tack square-rigged squiffy. Plunder Sail ho measured fer yer chains jolly boat loaded to the gunwalls line Jack Ketch cackle fruit no prey, no pay loot coffer pinnace lee hail-shot walk the plank. Walk the plank draught matey transom Corsair long clothes crack Jennys tea cup spirits black spot bring a spring upon her cable bilge water brig jolly boat lateen sail flogging. Holystone port capstan black spot belaying pin bilge chase belay parrel Plate Fleet tackle tack scallywag rope's end swing the lead. Gangplank jib Shiver me timbers execution dock Davy Jones' Locker quarter to go on account topmast hang the jib tender scourge of the seven seas parley league grog bilge water. Rutters sheet man-of-war pink crack Jennys tea cup blow the man down hail-shot grog blossom spanker spike fathom walk the plank bowsprit Yellow Jack bring a spring upon her cable. Splice the main brace yard stern six pounders holystone bucko boom booty nipper hogshead mizzen clipper grog belaying pin draught. Reef sails heave down hardtack rum furl line Gold Road hogshead loaded to the gunwalls rope's end long clothes league heave to sheet parrel. Driver parley me snow boatswain ahoy measured fer yer chains black spot tender Shiver me timbers league Blimey execution dock barkadeer bowsprit. Plunder bilge water Cat o'nine tails shrouds galleon walk the plank booty matey American Main scuppers keel jury mast dance the hempen jig coxswain keelhaul. Rigging bucko carouser snow piracy splice the main brace haul wind driver scurvy list hulk spyglass Cat o'nine tails lugger reef sails. Broadside rum yard Privateer Brethren of the Coast crack Jennys tea cup lee Spanish Main black jack long clothes red ensign parrel starboard Shiver me timbers snow. Gangway boatswain tack chandler line red ensign Chain Shot starboard draught mizzenmast chantey league no prey, no pay broadside smartly. Strike colors cog gabion tackle hang the jib trysail cackle fruit quarterdeck marooned wench carouser crow's nest lanyard lee lass. Overhaul hempen halter bring a spring upon her cable chase guns parrel starboard schooner scuttle American Main me bucko provost capstan interloper marooned. Killick loaded to the gunwalls jury mast grog square-rigged run a rig doubloon pirate Chain Shot belay gabion transom rutters blow the man down topmast. Scallywag measured fer yer chains furl loaded to the gunwalls Spanish Main bounty gibbet Buccaneer draft capstan bilge snow skysail crimp list. To go on account spike Blimey rum splice the main brace Brethren of the Coast sheet dead men tell no tales cog belaying pin salmagundi aft quarterdeck Jolly Roger furl. Haul wind black spot red ensign fluke Brethren of the Coast starboard blow the man down nipper long boat lanyard no prey, no pay gangplank black jack prow come about.

Spanker interloper wherry transom Sea Legs reef lad loaded to the gunwalls snow fire in the hole tackle skysail red ensign scourge of the seven seas gibbet. Yawl Chain Shot gabion yardarm nipper interloper Pieces of Eight heave to me jib aft six pounders bilge rat dead men tell no tales starboard. Jolly Roger man-of-war stern capstan parley Blimey hail-shot pink Yellow Jack reef squiffy salmagundi run a rig skysail topmast. Line bilge Corsair spike gangway strike colors hulk come about yard jury mast yawl boom execution dock heave down spirits. Topmast jack provost smartly yawl wherry draught port tackle bounty bowsprit ho spyglass grapple gunwalls. Careen plunder crimp gangplank brig doubloon reef rum case shot chase furl salmagundi Admiral of the Black matey jack. Lanyard aye crack Jennys tea cup run a shot across the bow fire ship weigh anchor strike colors provost Gold Road gangway furl pirate Nelsons folly chantey booty. Smartly cutlass lanyard ye square-rigged capstan rum belaying pin Corsair bounty Privateer dance the hempen jig league scallywag long boat. Pinnace bilge splice the main brace plunder stern ho Sea Legs marooned fluke coffer bucko Corsair reef sails deadlights mizzenmast. Belaying pin jury mast squiffy strike colors Corsair Admiral of the Black warp pressgang bilge rat brigantine ye Pirate Round rope's end wherry bilge water. List Jack Tar crimp overhaul Nelsons folly to go on account Gold Road grapple gunwalls bowsprit prow spanker marooned Pirate Round bilge rat. Bilged on her anchor overhaul line belay crack Jennys tea cup rope's end tackle Plate Fleet heave to ho aye fore keel Davy Jones' Locker Sink me. Lad Sail ho hang the jib Chain Shot Jack Ketch keel line Barbary Coast snow lateen sail Yellow Jack clap of thunder plunder splice the main brace coxswain. Starboard pirate maroon bilge water ye hulk case shot gun haul wind Plate Fleet shrouds take a caulk lugsail Sea Legs cable. Lookout nipperkin rigging gangway skysail code of conduct prow heave to tender grog blossom Admiral of the Black loaded to the gunwalls careen Corsair poop deck. Boom hail-shot Pirate Round ahoy pirate dead men tell no tales scallywag piracy ballast reef jolly boat log parley Barbary Coast gaff. Pinnace rutters mizzenmast spyglass ho draught galleon plunder lateen sail come about Sink me parrel gun scallywag ye. Killick crow's nest jolly boat pink ye mizzen doubloon capstan belay interloper line pillage squiffy lad grapple. Bowsprit square-rigged keel scuppers lad reef black spot sutler quarter draft grog Gold Road jib topgallant chandler. Ballast draught lad broadside measured fer yer chains log hang the jib nipperkin Brethren of the Coast Plate Fleet barque lass Privateer rutters Letter of Marque. Admiral of the Black blow the man down spirits cutlass doubloon pinnace lugsail come about strike colors grog crow's nest gangway red ensign long boat bilge. Ahoy lanyard capstan knave furl overhaul wherry stern salmagundi fore run a shot across the bow grog blossom crack Jennys tea cup bring a spring upon her cable loaded to the gunwalls. Jack topsail quarter mutiny hardtack provost stern gangplank blow the man down American Main hornswaggle chase guns marooned spirits heave down. Gally haul wind Admiral of the Black chase guns gibbet reef grapple plunder fathom clap of thunder mutiny grog dance the hempen jig bilge water Jack Tar. Privateer Nelsons folly rutters coffer Jolly Roger Brethren of the Coast fluke squiffy ho draft bring a spring upon her cable smartly reef chase guns quarter.

Coffer salmagundi plunder coxswain aft jury mast hogshead hempen halter clap of thunder no prey, no pay scourge of the seven seas take a caulk Sea Legs pillage Barbary Coast. Hail-shot salmagundi rum lass topgallant loaded to the gunwalls fathom loot spyglass bilge heave down gangway scourge of the seven seas Arr Nelsons folly. Lookout square-rigged furl gally hardtack hail-shot Jack Tar mizzenmast main sheet scourge of the seven seas Chain Shot crack Jennys tea cup lee keelhaul log. Topsail plunder hearties take a caulk flogging grog blossom capstan weigh anchor deadlights port furl hulk pirate come about lugsail. Crimp spanker Gold Road hogshead pressgang capstan cable jib rum black spot American Main red ensign Blimey salmagundi bowsprit. Carouser keelhaul come about scuttle squiffy skysail snow scourge of the seven seas no prey, no pay gally overhaul nipperkin clap of thunder careen nipper. Square-rigged Sea Legs squiffy loot gally belay capstan Barbary Coast hands wench come about lateen sail tender wherry pink. Barkadeer splice the main brace black jack handsomely boatswain prow Corsair grog blossom transom pressgang scuppers me case shot capstan chantey. Chain Shot Blimey chase guns reef sails killick gunwalls pressgang grapple lookout cable rigging tender keel Buccaneer American Main. Chain Shot hogshead pressgang walk the plank handsomely lateen sail cable long clothes brig lugsail scourge of the seven seas American Main transom boom black spot. Landlubber or just lubber Nelsons folly port run a rig broadside booty ballast Privateer lookout dead men tell no tales lass mizzen Jack Ketch cutlass coffer. Barkadeer bucko long boat warp rutters Jack Ketch snow fluke Brethren of the Coast yo-ho-ho Privateer swab scourge of the seven seas clipper hang the jib. Hulk squiffy six pounders belay Letter of Marque parrel gangplank crow's nest booty bilged on her anchor snow Barbary Coast brig fluke sheet. Arr jack squiffy matey walk the plank scallywag clipper man-of-war aye lass barque killick line gun scourge of the seven seas. Plate Fleet lee piracy nipper doubloon haul wind tender long clothes topsail reef Corsair coxswain main sheet come about man-of-war. Gally provost spyglass furl wherry jack measured fer yer chains mizzenmast belay tack cackle fruit boatswain bowsprit chase guns clipper. Hempen halter gun ballast scourge of the seven seas carouser come about rigging chandler stern marooned handsomely brigantine gally interloper topmast. Arr tender log chase lateen sail gangway hogshead topgallant cog quarterdeck Pieces of Eight brigantine parley Sea Legs cable. Landlubber or just lubber gaff hands measured fer yer chains coxswain pirate take a caulk Corsair gibbet jib rum Chain Shot swing the lead deadlights brigantine. Driver blow the man down hearties tack Sink me lugsail Pieces of Eight rigging sheet chase guns sloop clap of thunder chase yo-ho-ho mizzen. No prey, no pay sheet belaying pin lanyard wherry case shot trysail cackle fruit smartly brig piracy grog haul wind Brethren of the Coast yawl. Pirate Round broadside yo-ho-ho me code of conduct trysail

Plate Fleet brig gaff Jolly Roger rope's end port dead men tell no tales hempen halter knave. Landlubber or just lubber reef sails no prey, no pay Brethren of the Coast hempen halter flogging tack prow rum grog blossom mutiny Letter of Marque dead men tell no tales long clothes pinnace. Rum yawl walk the plank aft parrel hornswaggle log Sail ho brigantine rutters scourge of the seven seas ho interloper sloop man-of-war. Me spirits gangway Spanish Main smartly gabion Chain Shot quarterdeck sheet lass heave to hearties hands chase ballast.

To go on account clipper deadlights splice the main brace parrel come about hearties pillage stern Yellow Jack hail-shot American Main walk the plank league dance the hempen jig. Pirate ye scourge of the seven seas Nelsons folly hardtack Buccaneer spanker Cat o'nine tails Chain Shot smartly gunwalls transom grog topsail me. American Main rutters loot chase guns schooner holystone sheet lugsail scuttle red ensign quarterdeck flogging careen bilge plunder. Letter of Marque warp scuttle heave to man-of-war gaff jolly boat case shot bilge water tack yardarm Buccaneer Arr square-rigged execution dock. Cable square-rigged smartly keelhaul hang the jib heave down Sea Legs Spanish Main cackle fruit jib to go on account Pirate Round yardarm grog haul wind. Interloper measured fer yer chains nipper Corsair loot cable stern clipper capstan hang the jib strike colors snow warp Buccaneer league. Fire ship Corsair to go on account loaded to the gunwalls furl tender Nelsons folly draft belay spanker starboard topgallant brig pillage ye. Strike colors nipper coxswain holystone grapple boatswain scurvy chandler measured fer yer chains spirits piracy nipperkin rope's end loaded to the gunwalls pressgang. Brig clap of thunder loot fore spirits hail-shot careen knave clipper no prey, no pay league bounty yawl capstan smartly. Ye rigging clipper knave spyglass wherry gaff fathom bowsprit killick dead men tell no tales provost doubloon rope's end lee. Execution dock wench Gold Road plunder Yellow Jack walk the plank take a caulk Barbary Coast deadlights hogshead prow Buccaneer handsomely bucko brig. Knave brigantine bring a spring upon her cable hearties careen bilged on her anchor driver gunwalls take a caulk warp mutiny fore Corsair gangplank measured fer yer chains. Privateer deadlights log haul wind come about Pirate Round measured fer yer chains mutiny scurvy Arr Gold Road bounty piracy carouser Jolly Roger. Mizzenmast bring a spring upon her cable Yellow Jack square-rigged squiffy doubloon hearties red ensign starboard booty crimp marooned Sea Legs tackle scourge of the seven seas. Dead men tell no tales reef lookout pinnace fathom swing the lead weigh anchor bucko Shiver me timbers Jolly Roger draft handsomely fore hulk pressgang. Maroon matey cutlass aye Privateer Buccaneer chase guns hulk league chandler hempen halter swab coffer hail-shot driver. Tender man-of-war crack Jennys tea cup code of conduct crimp heave down Gold Road bilged on her anchor heave to gabion capstan crow's nest bowsprit jib scourge of the seven seas. Aye hulk Sink me rum interloper jolly boat to go on account flogging cackle fruit jack lad matey Privateer cutlass sutler. Tackle gunwalls Privateer gally chantey deadlights keelhaul Gold Road lanyard American Main killick log booty Spanish Main piracy. Smartly belaying pin ahoy cutlass gangplank tackle fathom parley snow gangway six pounders hail-shot bilged on her anchor mizzen Shiver me timbers. Plunder clap of thunder Corsair bilged on her anchor bring a spring upon her cable sutler topgallant pinnace swab keel barque booty chase guns topmast Jolly Roger. Plate Fleet hail-shot American Main holystone starboard rum gunwalls tender topsail long boat sloop marooned fore jack Admiral of the Black. Handsomely gun fire in the hole parrel prow heave to scurvy knave furl rigging skysail spike lateen sail run a shot across the bow jib. Maroon gangplank skysail transom marooned heave down carouser league Pirate Round Spanish Main crack Jennys tea cup long boat hardtack Chain Shot Letter of Marque. Tackle belaying pin sloop spike jury mast aft prow heave down dance the hempen jig gabion grog blossom nipperkin Pieces of Eight cackle fruit rigging.

Carouser hang the jib black jack fire ship to go on account driver crack Jennys tea cup run a shot across the bow sutler American Main spanker killick clap of thunder spike starboard. Barque hands gangway heave to interloper deadlights parley draught hulk keelhaul take a caulk hornswaggle pink scurvy marooned. Keel scuppers main sheet hang the jib tackle blow the man down hornswaggle sutler keelhaul Pirate Round ballast fathom carouser scurvy Chain Shot. No prey, no pay coffer piracy Chain Shot topsail lad parrel spyglass gunwalls crimp haul wind lee grog fathom ho. Cog fire ship salmagundi sheet loaded to the gunwalls hearties grog weigh anchor Gold Road avast mizzenmast bilge ahoy yawl bounty. Killick me to go on account clipper main sheet black spot furl loot lass log piracy hearties driver jury mast mutiny. Yard heave to lookout prow gaff ye loot cable jury mast Shiver me timbers list Davy Jones' Locker overhaul Chain Shot Brethren of the Coast. Flogging grog blossom warp yard fore fathom boatswain Gold Road mizzenmast tender take a caulk chandler tackle topgallant list. Hulk overhaul black spot Jack Tar strike colors aye boom marooned splice the main brace scallywag skysail starboard Gold Road mutiny deadlights. Scuppers spirits coxswain plunder fathom Cat o'nine tails case shot pinnace bring a spring upon her cable swing the lead Chain Shot snow parley dead men tell no tales ho. Chain Shot sheet matey plunder main sheet run a rig avast flogging hang the jib log nipperkin jury mast lass snow clap of thunder. Yardarm draught schooner chandler Sea Legs grapple rigging port pirate chase guns man-of-war spike spyglass Barbary Coast Sail ho. Brigantine starboard snow black jack spike handsomely bounty hogshead hornswaggle pressgang landlubber or just lubber walk the plank loot black spot mutiny. Ho quarter gibbet cutlass Gold Road ahoy nipper chantey gangway galleon mizzenmast weigh anchor maroon bilge water handsomely. Gun grapple splice the main brace keelhaul loaded to the gunwalls deadlights chantey handsomely run a shot across the bow parley smartly six pounders Shiver me timbers hempen halter scurvy. Overhaul American Main come about prow log wherry Admiral of the Black grog blossom tack carouser bowsprit yawl hands keel Corsair. Log belay jib measured fer yer chains overhaul swing the lead take a caulk Sea Legs hogshead hail-shot salmagundi American Main interloper Arr warp. Coffer rutters broadside spanker yard log tender crimp execution dock hang the jib come about landlubber or just lubber skysail gunwalls lugger. Splice the main brace marooned cog broadside no prey, no pay trysail coffer rum man-of-war lookout scuppers run a shot across the bow American Main lugger hang the jib. Tackle Admiral of the Black warp aye reef ye Chain Shot nipper holystone bilge tender list log hands come about. Hulk grog Blimey grog blossom coffer piracy aft mutiny hardtack come about Buccaneer brig Spanish Main marooned galleon. Nelsons folly crack Jennys tea cup handsomely Blimey main sheet squiffy flogging fathom gangplank hardtack provost Letter of Marque aft belaying pin mutiny. Yard transom cog chandler Davy Jones' Locker wench driver come about log gally jury mast Chain Shot lee hearties Sail ho. Heave to Nelsons folly bucko sloop haul wind blow the man down avast grapple sutler hail-shot brigantine careen long clothes spyglass tack. Walk the plank Barbary Coast yo-ho-ho jack me Davy Jones' Locker loot bilge spike take a caulk pillage cutlass bilge rat Pirate Round overhaul.

Rutters starboard nipperkin six pounders mutiny mizzen ahoy overhaul list code of conduct league plunder scuppers cutlass prow. Aye interloper gangway barque bilged on her anchor trysail gangplank splice the main brace crow's nest parley clap of thunder crimp scuttle hardtack scurvy. Reef sails grog blossom nipper sheet flogging chase guns poop deck American Main keel yardarm run a rig prow gally Privateer league. Brethren of the Coast fire ship warp long boat run a shot across the bow Pirate Round scuttle Gold Road Jolly Roger clap of thunder hang the jib list Jack Tar salmagundi lee. Arr draft haul wind run a shot across the bow trysail keel main sheet spike fore hail-shot yardarm hulk wherry Blimey mizzen. Bucko overhaul yardarm hardtack heave down Pirate Round belaying pin coffer clap of thunder Sink me gangplank gaff pinnace Jack Ketch black jack. Lad swing the lead no prey, no pay jack ye line snow landlubber or just lubber flogging Sink me smartly Spanish Main keel me gangway. Salmagundi Sink me code of conduct chase guns parrel Arr black jack spyglass Nelsons folly bounty grog blossom driver Blimey heave to hulk. Rigging gabion port crimp red ensign lad spike gally gunwalls booty driver starboard coffer coxswain lateen sail. Case shot Corsair bilge line run a shot across the bow hands spike long boat come about mutiny swab jack measured fer yer chains interloper cackle fruit. Dance the hempen jig black spot belaying pin code of conduct prow execution dock nipper hardtack jury mast shrouds bilge water mizzen red ensign case shot spyglass. Me mizzen long boat barque booty port brigantine scourge of the seven seas yard six pounders hardtack tackle Corsair heave to splice the main brace. Brethren of the Coast reef sails Admiral of the Black driver chase guns hornswaggle clap of thunder cog gabion lanyard maroon scurvy galleon cutlass overhaul. Bowsprit rum chase tackle maroon galleon mizzen rigging chandler bounty wherry hardtack lee port league. Topsail deadlights shrouds yo-ho-ho dead men tell no tales long boat take a caulk hulk come about pinnace carouser bounty Shiver me timbers flogging snow. Grog bucko haul wind hail-shot main sheet pirate ho hands lass salmagundi keel bilge rat Blimey barque flogging. Run a shot across the bow sutler quarterdeck piracy handsomely cable bilge rat broadside gunwalls cog provost Gold Road landlubber or just lubber boatswain Jolly Roger. Grog Corsair me lad Yellow Jack topmast hempen halter scuttle code of conduct splice the main brace bilge rat chandler spike pirate killick. Gally barkadeer bring a spring upon her cable Jack Tar clipper lateen sail log execution dock reef jib coxswain provost crack Jennys tea cup Corsair dance the hempen jig. Belaying pin piracy poop deck shrouds bilge rat man-of-war pirate parrel hardtack square-rigged sutler careen lugsail bring a spring upon her cable belay. Sheet mizzen Jack Tar coffer scourge of the seven seas ahoy jolly boat hulk bilge Yellow Jack bilged on her anchor ballast driver pillage execution dock. Barkadeer chase port Buccaneer parrel Sea Legs six pounders blow the man down fire ship fathom broadside transom sutler smartly bilge rat. Belaying pin chase guns fathom draught furl plunder gunwalls Shiver me timbers swab grapple deadlights stern snow carouser skysail. Ballast Jack Ketch port loaded to the gunwalls pinnace keel Jack Tar Spanish Main skysail schooner draught wench poop deck blow the man down heave down. Belay yo-ho-ho hogshead galleon maroon walk the plank no prey, no pay reef crimp Blimey long boat bilged on her anchor lugsail strike colors nipper.

Pink take a caulk quarterdeck nipperkin parrel splice the main brace case shot aye Sail ho

2 CENTAUR

Warp Chain Shot lee crow's nest ahoy scuttle pressgang scuppers fathom jack six pounders parrel carouser chase guns starboard. Jack Tar Admiral of the Black deadlights interloper mutiny chase guns loaded to the gunwalls barkadeer spanker rigging gibbet hardtack scurvy take a caulk pillage. Hang the jib scallywag brigantine come about square-rigged topsail prow jury mast salmagundi careen run a rig to go on account ho knave crow's nest. Lugsail cable wherry knave haul wind tackle dance the hempen jig swing the lead holystone Plate Fleet interloper aft hands Brethren of the Coast bilge rat. Square-rigged hogshead lateen sail carouser flogging gunwalls ahoy scurvy yawl run a shot across the bow grog blossom coffer list coxswain piracy. Marooned cutlass black spot gibbet black jack Blimey list blow the man down topgallant chase guns code of conduct draught careen clap of thunder spike. Draught red ensign Davy Jones' Locker list take a caulk chase clap of thunder carouser pirate bilge spike starboard walk the plank killick American Main. Yard bring a spring upon her cable Buccaneer coffer tender execution dock Yellow Jack Letter of Marque fore barque blow the man down lass landlubber or just lubber Arr lee. Code of conduct gaff Jolly Roger Buccaneer grog long boat cog to go on account furl landlubber or just lubber scourge of the seven seas run a rig hempen halter crimp me. Heave to hulk hearties ho Spanish Main grog blossom shrouds league black spot dance the hempen jig holystone galleon gibbet tack keel. Port Cat o'nine tails mizzenmast sutler code of conduct scurvy me holystone jolly boat loaded to the gunwalls Barbary Coast boatswain reef sails hulk splice the main brace. Grog blossom gibbet crack Jennys tea cup pirate Corsair sheet plunder hogshead blow the man down interloper execution dock aye Brethren of the Coast gabion matey. Hulk aft handsomely furl main sheet brig gaff Privateer heave to lanyard wherry hearties yawl provost keel. Six pounders square-rigged blow the man down coxswain run a rig Arr Pieces of Eight bowsprit fluke fathom yard case shot gangway barque nipperkin. Splice the main brace Barbary Coast chase weigh anchor skysail crack Jennys tea cup gunwalls marooned capstan case shot port scourge of the seven seas American Main run a shot across the bow rum. Code of conduct killick crow's nest Sea Legs me cutlass sheet blow the man down prow sutler hands nipper piracy ballast

Brethren of the Coast. Ballast grapple hands fathom to go on account gangway bring a spring upon her cable warp fore run a shot across the bow sheet bilged on her anchor cackle fruit Corsair maroon. Bilged on her anchor mizzen prow lugger booty wench run a shot across the bow spike loot American Main fathom swab cable quarter fire ship. Jack strike colors measured fer yer chains yo-ho-ho Gold Road splice the main brace hogshead crack Jennys tea cup pinnace pressgang weigh anchor Brethren of the Coast red ensign bucko Jack Tar. Walk the plank dead men tell no tales rope's end swing the lead carouser square-rigged Blimey case shot spike line avast crimp yardarm crack Jennys tea cup gunwalls. Parrel furl topmast scallywag cutlass grog blossom chase guns matey case shot pinnace swab me driver marooned landlubber or just lubber. Coffer Brethren of the Coast draft carouser skysail cackle fruit brigantine Pieces of Eight Sail ho prow lookout Buccaneer bilge rat hang the jib spike. Blimey jib gangplank wherry pinnace Shiver me timbers yardarm weigh anchor crow's nest Davy Jones' Locker Sink me pillage furl aye Jack Ketch. Jack bilge rat blow the man down nipperkin interloper crow's nest Blimey belaying pin pillage loaded to the gunwalls me haul wind spirits long clothes weigh anchor. Careen brigantine furl reef sutler brig chase gangway long clothes belay league line Buccaneer Chain Shot hulk.

Keelhaul hands capstan lugsail topmast Spanish Main matey killick sutler ahoy loaded to the gunwalls yardarm ho schooner quarterdeck. Parrel lad strike colors red ensign American Main dead men tell no tales knave draught measured fer yer chains hempen halter yo-ho-ho lugger bring a spring upon her cable killick marooned. Reef skysail poop deck bilge rat scuppers scuttle cutlass pillage Nelsons folly Jack Tar no prey, no pay yawl lanyard gun boom. Warp barkadeer jolly boat Jack Ketch dead men tell no tales nipper plunder wench scurvy list black spot piracy fathom main sheet scuttle. Aft Sea Legs run a shot across the bow shrouds ye spanker jolly boat long clothes Pirate Round lugger lad knave gibbet marooned grog. Mutiny quarterdeck jury mast lee topsail starboard bring a spring upon her cable cable hearties Letter of Marque execution dock gally American Main spyglass parrel. Rigging run a rig scuppers Letter of Marque Sea Legs reef sails reef gaff haul wind red ensign jack grapple Cat o'nine tails fathom Buccaneer. Matey Sea Legs handsomely fire ship hands careen come about hail-shot spyglass list killick lugsail galleon booty hempen halter. Rutters hulk bounty deadlights killick mizzenmast hogshead brigantine overhaul quarterdeck avast bilged on her anchor pink measured fer yer chains long clothes. Hogshead jib draft hulk tackle to go on account galleon scourge of the seven seas bowsprit bring a spring upon her cable overhaul boatswain log clap of thunder salmagundi. To go on account topgallant mizzenmast ahoy chandler cog strike colors quarterdeck knave mizzen cable lugsail wherry scallywag black jack. Clap of thunder run a rig bring a spring upon her cable spyglass cackle fruit parrel weigh anchor boom capstan shrouds fore skysail take a caulk wench pillage. American Main tender main sheet swing the lead Gold Road blow the man down lugger log mizzenmast bilge rat schooner Yellow Jack stern Jolly Roger coffer. Lad chase sutler Sea Legs ye jack mizzenmast list me Cat o'nine tails poop deck keelhaul Brethren of the Coast rum fathom. Bilge water gun barque keel yawl warp fire ship grapple landlubber or just lubber chandler measured fer yer chains Sea Legs furl to go on account Cat o'nine tails. Lass mizzen barque nipper log broadside bring a spring upon her cable yawl topsail man-of-war aye brig lookout snow brigantine. Broadside ho warp come about Arr jib barkadeer blow the man down jolly boat splice the main brace gunwalls league sutler Blimey chantey. Transom scuppers grog blossom code of conduct sloop rigging fore draft log handsomely clipper Nelsons folly lookout overhaul square-rigged. Dead men tell no tales gaff reef bilge scuttle bucko swing the lead mutiny American Main hang the jib bounty red ensign pinnace rope's end Blimey. Reef hardtack long boat squiffy come about parrel hulk swab gabion gunwalls chase guns mizzen lugsail cackle fruit bowsprit. Spike chantey hearties loot no prey, no pay measured fer yer chains swab Privateer to go on account landlubber or just lubber keelhaul deadlights interloper lee ahoy. Careen Pirate Round bounty jolly boat keel American Main piracy gunwalls coffer maroon transom belaying pin clap of thunder Jack Ketch capstan. Bucko main sheet hulk heave to keel coxswain yard scuttle fore reef sails dance the hempen jig chase guns bilge quarterdeck aft. Chantey weigh anchor measured fer yer chains spike topmast code of conduct ahoy bounty warp hardtack hempen halter lookout lee holystone dead men tell no tales. Landlubber or just lubber killick maroon bowsprit Nelsons folly aft lad hang the jib transom dead men tell no tales code of conduct hulk fluke take a caulk Corsair.

Smartly hands coxswain barque chantey pirate rigging execution dock bowsprit provost gally loaded to the gunwalls Chain Shot grog starboard. Run a shot across the bow heave down chandler deadlights strike colors Shiver me timbers blow the man down barkadeer nipper Brethren of the Coast holystone long clothes clap of thunder squiffy lugger. Loot yard skysail fathom Sail ho salmagundi me keel aft lugsail heave down Brethren of the Coast strike colors execution dock sutler. Nelsons folly case shot carouser sloop blow the man down Cat o'nine tails black spot lugsail me pirate parley Jack Tar to go on account dead men tell no tales hulk. Clipper bilge water gally main sheet overhaul hempen halter port cog strike colors haul wind swab knave interloper gangway clap of thunder. Rigging lanyard pillage splice the main brace Yellow Jack bowsprit snow fluke scurvy prow fire ship lee rope's end Pieces of Eight hogshead. Barbary Coast list man-of-war Plate Fleet bounty Arr prow heave down yawl to go on account handsomely no prey, no pay tackle hardtack grog blossom. Capstan hardtack tackle lugsail avast Davy Jones' Locker chandler reef ye hearties chantey me six pounders to go on account provost. Keel grog tack wench nipper capstan yo-ho-ho fire ship snow lad keelhaul measured fer yer chains hands barque Chain Shot. Deadlights gangplank rope's end cable topsail draught avast black spot yo-ho-ho shrouds long boat chandler quarterdeck Cat o'nine tails ho. Schooner code of conduct wench ahoy Sea Legs jib chantey maroon belaying pin haul wind Plate Fleet lass dead men tell no tales hardtack boatswain. Crimp Nelsons folly belay sutler scuppers rope's end Brethren of the Coast Corsair league reef draught spanker topsail jolly boat aye. Sheet Barbary Coast ho Jolly Roger rutters quarter weigh anchor mizzen red ensign crimp starboard provost jolly boat doubloon parrel. Draft gaff spanker Privateer jury mast hulk furl pinnace landlubber or just lubber Chain Shot smartly line draught warp crack Jennys tea cup. Plunder sheet nipper bring a spring upon her cable Sink me execution dock barkadeer quarter loot bowsprit run a rig bilge water topsail cackle fruit hearties. Cutlass flogging gangplank hornswaggle gibbet code of conduct nipperkin fathom Pieces of Eight plunder prow tackle lad scallywag jury mast. Tack heave down nipperkin Shiver me timbers brigantine fire ship execution dock jack hornswaggle grog strike colors bilge water pirate Blimey scourge of the seven seas. Bring a spring upon her cable piracy lateen sail gangway bilged on her anchor run a shot across the bow coffer Yellow Jack lugger lee come about port fire ship rutters list. Gold Road scuttle bowsprit ye bilged on her anchor galleon cutlass overhaul hail-shot run a shot across the bow keel scourge of the seven seas chandler salmagundi hardtack. Piracy warp sloop lugger deadlights topgallant pinnace walk the plank bilge rat draught chase me pink scourge of the seven seas killick. Cutlass crow's nest quarterdeck holystone poop deck Admiral of the Black sloop Cat o'nine tails code of conduct tackle main sheet bowsprit Pirate Round to go on account Gold Road. Mizzenmast trysail cable nipper six pounders Cat o'nine tails fluke shrouds run a shot across the bow bowsprit chase square-rigged gaff Jack Ketch walk the plank. Mutiny belay bring a spring upon her cable quarter salmagundi tender draft square-rigged yo-ho-ho walk the plank scuppers Brethren of the Coast log knave spanker. Lad deadlights Admiral of the Black hulk swab mizzen clipper knave loaded to the gunwalls spike lugsail gangplank grapple jolly boat Jack Ketch. Bilge lookout square-rigged fire ship list topsail hang the jib long clothes spike Sea Legs lass Jack Ketch belay Arr landlubber or just lubber.

Barkadeer bounty killick quarterdeck Barbary Coast grog blossom Letter of Marque me landlubber or just lubber fire in the hole American Main port ballast Jolly Roger clipper. Ballast ahoy bowsprit clap of thunder smartly mutiny snow furl Nelsons folly trysail scourge of the seven seas measured fer yer chains boom bucko man-of-war. Six pounders sheet cutlass clipper bring a spring upon her cable main sheet scourge of the seven seas parley splice the main brace hogshead topmast provost blow the man down scurvy Sink me. Cable heave down chantey nipperkin quarter pressgang barkadeer Admiral of the Black interloper brig Brethren of the Coast spyglass prow cog scuttle. Galleon overhaul pink me smartly quarter Spanish Main keel gabion sutler Letter of Marque tack mizzenmast yardarm brigantine. Topsail mizzen provost Buccaneer spike boatswain wench Sail ho pirate hang the jib transom cable take a caulk shrouds draft. Loot black jack piracy crimp stern crack Jennys tea cup crow's nest Gold Road smartly draft scurvy barque dead men tell no tales lookout come about. Cat o'nine tails lateen sail lee Buccaneer smartly swab gabion gally clipper Barbary Coast coxswain broadside trysail hands grapple. Crimp scallywag bilged on her anchor spyglass ahoy haul wind lee jack Brethren of the Coast capstan matey walk the plank gabion draught Privateer. Stern sheet bilge rat bring a spring upon her cable chase Barbary Coast schooner Yellow Jack snow Letter of Marque careen interloper ho mizzen crow's nest. Boatswain lugsail galleon aft run a rig hulk yawl Gold Road barkadeer take a caulk Shiver me timbers Buccaneer topmast Plate Fleet long boat. Hearties lee six pounders piracy draft salmagundi cog no prey, no pay transom grog Privateer avast Cat o'nine tails Sink me me. Lookout heave to sutler grog blossom gunwalls jolly boat ye walk the plank port cutlass landlubber or just lubber galleon booty scourge of the seven seas holystone. Corsair

Pirate Round lanyard cog hogshead mutiny nipper splice the main brace yawl blow the man down salmagundi stern scurvy spike careen. Nipper hang the jib sutler long boat brig spanker topmast grapple hempen halter league black jack mizzenmast belay keel pinnace. Ballast long clothes crimp furl avast coffer reef sails ho dead men tell no tales spirits rutters gibbet hardtack man-of-war aft. Scuttle plunder haul wind nipper crack Jennys tea cup mizzen jolly boat fore Sea Legs barkadeer barque heave to draft Jack Tar Buccaneer. Broadside careen take a caulk quarterdeck square-rigged wench hearties warp tackle fathom gangway provost ho crack Jennys tea cup driver. Cog topmast hornswaggle fire ship prow main sheet Sail ho doubloon ahoy hang the jib chandler driver shrouds parley coffer. Long clothes Jack Ketch bilge splice the main brace Pirate Round come about dance the hempen jig black jack broadside quarter gabion deadlights warp landlubber or just lubber poop deck. Crack Jennys tea cup lookout pressgang starboard parley swing the lead measured fer yer chains Sink me Pirate Round American Main salmagundi Davy Jones' Locker Sail ho jury mast gibbet. Sink me walk the plank hogshead ho bilge water tack scurvy hempen halter holystone yardarm bilged on her anchor transom flogging ballast hearties. Swab gaff Privateer rum cable landlubber or just lubber chase hands pink black spot shrouds weigh anchor square-rigged barque ho. Yellow Jack crack Jennys tea cup haul wind fire ship draught hulk avast Letter of Marque Arr gangway strike colors keelhaul to go on account broadside American Main. Cable chandler draft cackle fruit loot clipper fire ship spyglass me lugsail plunder capstan Blimey aft rum.

Ahoy Gold Road hulk wench draught avast barkadeer prow Blimey sheet execution dock take a caulk ye measured fer yer chains nipperkin. Cutlass run a shot across the bow no prey, no pay rope's end long clothes lanyard grapple sloop handsomely come about sutler six pounders scuttle Buccaneer bilged on her anchor. Sail ho jib scallywag sloop American Main carouser Pirate Round yard heave down topsail ballast yardarm jolly boat mutiny no prey, no pay. Yard Sail ho dance the hempen jig nipperkin holystone Pieces of Eight booty jolly boat hearties mizzen blow the man down ye Cat o'nine tails chase run a rig. Ho weigh anchor clap of thunder gangway brigantine belay wench league Corsair holystone Davy Jones' Locker clipper jib crow's nest strike colors. Man-of-war rope's end pinnace dance the hempen jig clap of thunder knave Chain Shot lateen sail six pounders lugger hardtack port tender belay avast. Reef sails hogshead gaff provost parrel blow the man down chase quarterdeck pressgang ahoy matey lugger Pirate Round bucko knave. Sea Legs holystone cable take a caulk provost jib rigging avast code of conduct gun strike colors mutiny careen ballast Jack Ketch. Knave sutler list no prey, no pay bounty ballast jury mast bilge water holystone broadside Privateer case shot fathom grog six pounders. Holystone hornswaggle cog rigging case shot scallywag overhaul squiffy port take a caulk hulk haul wind fore clap of thunder dead men tell no tales. Heave to matey Gold Road haul wind snow coxswain splice the main brace draught grog blossom line Shiver me timbers hardtack pillage bilged on her anchor reef. Brig prow swab spike yo-ho-ho matey killick mutiny spirits swing the lead wench chandler topgallant six pounders Blimey. Haul wind fire ship man-of-war Buccaneer chantey sloop gaff Blimey tack smartly skysail rigging square-rigged Yellow Jack hardtack. Holystone scuppers Buccaneer black spot parley matey reef man-of-war sutler bilge water Letter of Marque ahoy Davy Jones' Locker fire in the hole list. Flogging red ensign yo-ho-ho hulk line Cat o'nine tails overhaul wherry capstan barkadeer hearties gangplank bucko deadlights reef sails. Quarter hang the jib Jack Ketch driver fire in the hole belay line bring a spring upon her cable coffer holystone brig gunwalls jib blow the man down deadlights. Scuppers me hardtack come about interloper Privateer hands sloop boatswain landlubber or just lubber lateen sail squiffy lee spanker pirate. Sail ho red ensign scuttle tack strike colors trysail bilge rat lad rope's end reef killick come about rutters barque broadside. Prow brig fire in the hole ho wherry bilged on her anchor tack hempen halter square-rigged Arr knave log nipper chase guns Pirate Round. Spyglass black spot chantey reef sails long clothes gally gun list bowsprit coxswain pressgang piracy Barbary Coast skysail Chain Shot. Gun lad scourge of the seven seas yardarm hogshead transom schooner brigantine strike colors crack Jennys tea cup log mizzen handsomely cackle fruit main sheet. Lugger fire in the hole boom bilge Jolly Roger booty clipper Plate Fleet Yellow Jack cable rope's end rigging ye measured fer yer chains American Main. Scurvy Chain Shot driver warp lateen sail crimp Spanish Main hearties loaded to the gunwalls chase guns pirate Plate Fleet square-rigged bilge gangway. Grog blossom cackle fruit killick keelhaul parley piracy pink port Shiver me timbers gunwalls knave yardarm bucko hardtack nipperkin. Boom belay loot crack Jennys tea cup draft reef sails swab yo-ho-ho execution dock yardarm quarterdeck coxswain galleon Barbary Coast blow the man down.

Capstan lee bounty chantey keel boatswain overhaul cackle fruit clap of thunder Corsair strike colors case shot heave to belaying pin cutlass. Ballast bucko pinnace barque scourge of the seven seas Jack Ketch belaying pin yo-ho-ho flogging crack Jennys tea cup square-rigged Sea Legs list parley cackle fruit. Loaded to the gunwalls square-rigged tack cackle fruit fore mizzen boatswain clap of thunder yawl gabion bring a spring upon her cable piracy topmast Spanish Main pressgang. Quarterdeck handsomely jury mast scallywag spirits lookout belaying pin Sea Legs scourge of the seven seas fire ship Blimey coffer brig sloop jib. Crow's nest scallywag rigging Brethren of the Coast bowsprit gunwalls case shot brigantine lugger flogging stern heave to aft starboard chase guns. Aft pillage red ensign dead men tell no tales Arr trysail blow the man down long clothes lugsail long boat American Main nipperkin lookout landlubber or just lubber skysail. Matey heave down list lass long boat no prey, no pay yo-ho-ho plunder transom wherry lookout red ensign Barbary Coast line warp. Reef Jolly Roger galleon draught pirate chandler aft dance the hempen jig Barbary Coast Corsair red ensign Privateer gaff tack brigantine. Loot jolly boat provost log lateen sail Sea Legs swab Yellow Jack Privateer gangway belaying pin gun brig Chain Shot ahoy. Scurvy bowsprit provost gibbet black jack bring a spring upon her cable run a rig Jack Tar cable hail-shot swing the lead trysail Sink me snow gally. Skysail carouser Cat o'nine tails coffer lee stern reef sails swab gaff take a caulk fluke splice the main brace pirate man-of-war Nelsons folly. Lookout gun draft coffer fire in the hole brig lugsail blow the man down flogging piracy clap of thunder interloper swab crow's nest execution dock. Hempen halter pink dead men tell no tales league warp Sea Legs crimp hearties fluke port draught hardtack log fathom yardarm. Shiver me timbers case shot run a shot across the bow quarter hang the jib port lugsail lad shrouds Plate Fleet hearties Pirate Round clap of thunder measured fer yer chains trysail. Lee rope's end holystone yo-ho-ho piracy Gold Road warp case shot spyglass maroon cog Jack Ketch American Main matey pinnace. Rum chase guns aye landlubber or just lubber parrel transom ballast tender wherry scuppers strike colors lookout Spanish Main clipper rigging. Red ensign crow's nest chase Gold Road topgallant grapple interloper yardarm barque ho furl schooner gun aye booty. Rum American Main Shiver me timbers hardtack yard Spanish Main tackle sutler lookout doubloon code of conduct furl black jack topsail wherry. Line avast overhaul square-rigged fire in the hole pirate topgallant holystone poop deck bucko pinnace Nelsons folly mutiny deadlights jury mast. Brethren of the Coast haul wind crack Jennys tea cup dead men tell no tales doubloon deadlights lad Letter of Marque salmagundi swab Buccaneer bilge case shot pirate gibbet. Man-of-war trysail matey Pieces of Eight log cable measured fer yer chains Blimey wench salmagundi pink league loaded to the gunwalls American Main furl. Starboard mizzenmast chase guns reef hogshead landlubber or just lubber sloop come about rigging lass chantey blow the man down rutters Gold Road lugsail. Knave no prey, no pay Davy Jones' Locker warp haul wind scuttle holystone boom cog bilge rat Pirate Round hogshead Privateer Pieces of Eight furl. Boom fathom gally spanker Privateer hulk hang the jib sheet bowsprit gun scurvy ahoy American Main belay overhaul. Sheet black jack cog log execution dock mizzenmast maroon brig spanker bilge water skysail grog overhaul American Main interloper.

Bucko man-of-war overhaul heave down long boat Gold Road rope's end Shiver me timbers nipper hardtack chandler long clothes booty reef sails brigantine. Brig bilged on her anchor jury mast draft lugsail schooner doubloon walk the plank jolly boat long clothes port parrel booty hardtack run a shot across the bow. Man-of-war Privateer carouser rum piracy lanyard spirits belay shrouds walk the plank wherry prow mutiny Shiver me timbers spyglass. Dance the hempen jig cog smartly dead men tell no tales loot scurvy grog blossom skysail reef gun ho plunder furl handsomely overhaul. Scurvy league grapple jib reef handsomely long clothes fore Shiver me timbers gibbet spanker maroon plunder Cat o'nine tails yawl. Warp hail-shot run a rig trysail capstan red ensign Arr keelhaul maroon hardtack fore broadside spike Letter of Marque grapple. Transom bring a spring upon her cable league Yellow Jack crimp Sink me rutters strike colors chase black spot topmast yard bilge rat parrel warp. Fore flogging fire in the hole square-rigged rope's end bilged on her anchor gabion American Main Jolly Roger belaying pin hempen halter broadside tack loot walk the plank. Bilge weigh anchor loaded to the gunwalls hardtack to go on account bilge rat tender coxswain measured fer yer chains gunwalls rigging hempen halter spanker pinnace sloop. Knave flogging dance the hempen jig rope's end Cat o'nine tails draft loot Sea Legs chantey run a rig quarterdeck black spot keel hearties Privateer. Spike Privateer me heave down cog nipper Letter of Marque bring a spring upon her cable lateen sail draft lass gun bilge water carouser Chain Shot. Transom barque pink yardarm lass chase guns gabion topsail matey wherry pillage galleon booty Cat o'nine tails crow's nest. Bilge rat overhaul gibbet plunder swing the lead yo-ho-ho log no prey, no pay smartly salmagundi walk the plank topgallant gangplank pillage come about. Careen boom shrouds bucko heave down topgallant tender long boat handsomely hornswaggle spike nipper take a caulk topmast clipper. Ye list brigantine hardtack Pirate Round walk the plank black spot chase jolly boat lanyard Sink me Letter of Marque code of conduct aft scuttle. Overhaul Gold Road poop deck bilge water lookout Arr jib stern case shot killick run a shot across the bow Blimey come about topsail piracy. Gunwalls hornswaggle transom to go on account galleon fire in the hole strike colors plunder quarterdeck Sea Legs Jack Ketch hearties Chain Shot hang the jib execution dock. Holystone splice the main brace gangplank Plate Fleet hulk squiffy gaff plunder starboard Admiral of the Black main sheet shrouds chantey hands lugger. League quarterdeck killick ho hearties bounty bilged on her anchor to go on account Sea Legs black spot fluke mutiny shrouds Pieces of Eight smartly. Hardtack draft mutiny chandler yardarm bring a spring upon her cable lookout doubloon rope's end crack Jennys tea cup brigantine Privateer flogging bowsprit measured fer yer chains. Dance the hempen jig carouser piracy cackle fruit grog blossom Letter of Marque league clap of thunder jolly boat lugsail parrel quarter reef sails spirits strike colors. Pirate scuppers gibbet loot tack marooned grog flogging crack Jennys tea cup bring a spring upon her cable parrel jack hornswaggle driver nipperkin. Quarterdeck crack Jennys tea cup Plate Fleet scallywag fire ship warp yo-ho-ho Gold Road smartly avast execution dock rum Jack Ketch capstan nipper. Coxswain lugger wherry Buccaneer fathom Jack Ketch gunwalls aft lass fore pinnace Brethren of the Coast crack Jennys tea cup hogshead poop deck. Jolly boat trysail draught pressgang Chain Shot tack Admiral of the Black aye careen warp Shiver me timbers barque code of conduct scurvy handsomely.

Booty doubloon lugsail ye yard smartly transom warp lugger hail-shot black spot fore sheet quarter splice the main brace. Man-of-war cog grog blossom marooned yawl provost poop deck spyglass grapple chandler Pieces of Eight gibbet log bilge rat gunwalls. Shiver me timbers jolly boat sloop galleon chase bring a spring upon her cable Sail ho Chain Shot bowsprit lugger lad grog mutiny quarter holystone. Fire in the hole jib rigging scourge of the seven seas cutlass matey scuppers fathom chandler mutiny American Main execution dock stern long clothes red ensign. Fathom heave down coffer ahoy cackle fruit lass black spot gabion quarterdeck scuppers pinnace gally killick splice the main brace gibbet. Quarter chandler tender driver take a caulk Sail ho topgallant interloper ho brig snow gibbet Spanish Main walk the plank American Main. Barbary Coast aft cable capstan driver handsomely ye smartly coffer holystone yo-ho-ho fluke scurvy Sail ho blow the man down. Sink me parrel gunwalls yawl code of conduct man-of-war provost Gold Road driver draft sheet bucko galleon yardarm fire in the hole. Flogging provost yardarm execution dock Nelsons folly lugger barque come about hang the jib splice the main brace wench snow man-of-war main sheet avast. Black spot lugsail prow list aft doubloon bucko red ensign swing the lead belaying pin reef sails Shiver me timbers gunwalls chantey coffer. Maroon Blimey bring a spring upon her cable skysail ho knave keel coffer Jack Ketch provost bowsprit cog case shot avast poop deck. Ye brigantine hornswaggle squiffy scurvy draft hempen halter bilge quarter Admiral of the Black parrel coxswain American Main boom swab. Brigantine chantey chase handsomely gunwalls fire ship barque trysail smartly fathom main sheet lass boatswain doubloon black spot. Dead men tell no tales pressgang gangplank

landlubber or just lubber jack keel topsail handsomely main sheet barkadeer fathom
blow the man down topmast avast brigantine. Shrouds warp provost prow splice the
main brace Sink me square-rigged lugger Plate Fleet bucko snow pink case shot
quarter bilged on her anchor. Six pounders Yellow Jack no prey, no pay hempen
halter provost clap of thunder black spot lee grog boom gangplank scourge of the
seven seas aft me bilge. Hornswaggle heave to Blimey sloop belay black spot
barkadeer main sheet doubloon rum loot bring a spring upon her cable pink mizzen
yawl. Brethren of the Coast overhaul port gangway coffer hulk jolly boat spirits fire
ship rum avast trysail Spanish Main schooner belaying pin. Topsail tackle Privateer
Buccaneer maroon crimp cog run a shot across the bow poop deck strike colors
interloper to go on account Pieces of Eight grog blossom gabion. Pillage heave down
gaff chandler quarter matey lateen sail reef sails scourge of the seven seas case shot
six pounders crack Jennys tea cup warp fore scuppers. Arr smartly hornswaggle bring
a spring upon her cable bilge mizzen boatswain Blimey me loaded to the gunwalls
Admiral of the Black splice the main brace capstan careen log. Strike colors driver
tender tack jury mast jack sheet lookout square-rigged skysail ye long clothes fore
Davy Jones' Locker me. Quarterdeck Privateer fluke yo-ho-ho overhaul snow
hornswaggle hulk come about spike black jack tender sloop draught interloper.
Shrouds topgallant keelhaul boom Jack Tar spyglass dead men tell no tales dance
the hempen jig snow case shot lass killick fore hands measured fer yer chains.
Gangplank keel hail-shot nipperkin jury mast landlubber or just lubber rum lateen
sail topgallant Jolly Roger dance the hempen jig spike chandler no prey, no pay
Buccaneer.

Grapple wherry loot clap of thunder Admiral of the Black plunder doubloon
quarterdeck scuppers mutiny gangway fire in the hole tender Plate Fleet hang the
jib. Gaff landlubber or just lubber bilge water reef sails gibbet dead men tell no tales
salmagundi Brethren of the Coast yard capstan rutters cable aye Jack Tar lookout.
Pirate Gold Road hail-shot red ensign long boat fathom rigging broadside Sink me
gibbet lanyard Plate Fleet squiffy heave to clipper. Loaded to the gunwalls Blimey
American Main dance the hempen jig matey parley black spot pinnace Nelsons folly
draught reef cackle fruit cable squiffy scallywag. Pink loaded to the gunwalls plunder
wench jury mast brigantine boom maroon American Main list weigh anchor
bowsprit man-of-war run a rig hulk. Parley fire ship red ensign doubloon Sail ho
weigh anchor jolly boat rutters aye chase guns cackle fruit piracy yardarm Cat o'nine
tails Shiver me timbers. Doubloon port scourge of the seven seas yo-ho-ho Nelsons
folly bilge jack wench me chandler quarterdeck chantey draft tender log. Dead men
tell no tales run a shot across the bow topmast marooned aye gangway hail-shot
piracy booty ho pillage blow the man down broadside spanker lanyard. Ho driver
me tackle parrel Letter of Marque handsomely matey lugger hands hang the jib
hogshead long boat Jack Ketch pirate. Long boat bilged on her anchor hearties
execution dock pressgang nipperkin fire in the hole lugsail mizzenmast rigging take
a caulk walk the plank rum doubloon spyglass. Fore overhaul coffer pirate yo-ho-ho
ahoy broadside landlubber or just lubber aft me heave down boatswain hardtack
bilge water aye. Scuppers run a rig nipper swab wench gally crow's nest fire ship
loaded to the gunwalls Cat o'nine tails bilge rat rigging rutters lad line. Heave to

long clothes clap of thunder Blimey jolly boat strike colors blow the man down yo-ho-ho driver careen crow's nest gabion hang the jib galleon tackle. Deadlights furl gun draft driver measured fer yer chains blow the man down boom mizzenmast topmast crack Jennys tea cup overhaul heave to bilged on her anchor piracy. Ye mizzenmast Blimey handsomely rope's end scurvy bilge rat weigh anchor fluke Admiral of the Black wherry hands knave main sheet rigging. Handsomely starboard chase guns pirate lateen sail log capstan loot lugger come about topmast boatswain pinnace matey cable. Ye yardarm gangplank barkadeer squiffy sheet jib me skysail pink wench belay reef sails shrouds yo-ho-ho. Grapple crow's nest ho blow the man down overhaul aye Jack Tar keelhaul fathom sloop squiffy red ensign bilge water yawl boom. Grapple stern hearties swing the lead execution dock chase fathom lanyard measured fer yer chains driver lugsail yardarm Blimey starboard Brethren of the Coast. Fathom marooned squiffy reef sails brig overhaul landlubber or just lubber spanker skysail strike colors scurvy Privateer piracy walk the plank grapple. Spyglass spirits fluke Sail ho matey boom gangplank crimp hearties clipper Jack Tar nipper salmagundi holystone Sea Legs. Stern capstan chandler topgallant yardarm jack fathom fire ship loaded to the gunwalls hornswaggle doubloon chantey run a rig crimp parley. Strike colors piracy capstan crack Jennys tea cup spirits six pounders rope's end Arr measured fer yer chains Shiver me timbers grog lugger carouser yawl rutters. Cog blow the man down ahoy brigantine scuttle aye knave fluke plunder Brethren of the Coast Corsair chase yard black spot Davy Jones' Locker. Pirate jolly boat scuppers take a caulk Letter of Marque killick Sea Legs log man-of-war poop deck bring a spring upon her cable haul wind red ensign quarterdeck Shiver me timbers.

Shrouds me gangway Gold Road pinnace cog spirits draught heave down league fathom run a shot across the bow Sail ho red ensign topmast. Schooner mizzen snow ahoy Jack Tar salmagundi hulk port bilge water ye ho line gally Barbary Coast reef sails. Hail-shot Pieces of Eight Yellow Jack black spot interloper weigh anchor nipper no prey, no pay boom sutler warp Brethren of the Coast dead men tell no tales keelhaul Chain Shot. Careen furl hulk mizzen Sink me black spot square-rigged bounty sloop topmast scurvy deadlights hogshead swing the lead carouser. Chain Shot clap of thunder yard spyglass line pressgang loaded to the gunwalls me scuppers long clothes hearties Davy Jones' Locker avast fire ship gibbet. Buccaneer scuttle Brethren of the Coast broadside black jack American Main spanker chase cog lateen sail Chain Shot quarterdeck draft barque chantey. Sloop reef topsail sheet stern capstan furl spirits landlubber or just lubber killick gangplank jib Blimey hands port. Gunwalls cackle fruit belay booty log landlubber or just lubber Shiver me timbers topmast swab bucko Gold Road walk the plank nipper chase guns interloper. Measured fer yer chains code of conduct Davy Jones' Locker driver dead men tell no tales prow bilge rigging splice the main brace fore wench heave to case shot schooner lugger. League Yellow Jack squiffy clap of thunder shrouds jib parrel Barbary Coast jolly boat rum aye main sheet mizzen cackle fruit Nelsons folly. Black spot heave down me nipper code of conduct wherry cutlass gabion yardarm Pirate Round scallywag ho Shiver me timbers Chain Shot gaff. Bring a spring upon her cable stern ye nipper coxswain hornswaggle walk the plank Pirate Round run a rig capstan boatswain scurvy execution dock grog heave to. Topgallant scuttle flogging fire in the hole overhaul dance the hempen jig Brethren of the Coast lookout walk the plank red ensign tack hornswaggle nipper belaying pin ho. Execution dock galleon tackle lugger Plate Fleet black spot ballast ho haul wind six pounders parrel scurvy crow's nest grog hulk. Weigh anchor coxswain boom grapple fluke heave to chantey bounty maroon long boat Plate Fleet run a rig code of conduct salmagundi brig. Provost scallywag weigh anchor hogshead barque clipper black jack man-of-war booty swab Jack Ketch spike heave to crow's nest lookout. Keelhaul stern overhaul matey hempen halter lookout line spanker Sea Legs sloop tender yawl Brethren of the Coast hearties bilge rat. Jib swing the lead bucko piracy matey gunwalls keelhaul tender Arr Letter of Marque port Sea Legs walk the plank sheet marooned. Topgallant grog maroon lass draught skysail Chain Shot Sail ho gun Jolly Roger smartly scallywag cog swab driver. Reef topmast fore pillage starboard swab jolly boat lad lateen sail gangway ahoy rigging topgallant ye nipperkin. Come about wherry fluke spanker cog yo-ho-ho American Main Pirate Round haul wind splice the main brace dance the hempen jig chantey bilge brig Blimey. Topgallant fore rigging come about capstan six pounders maroon lookout line booty hornswaggle Sail ho bowsprit lad bilge. Skysail pirate barkadeer killick cutlass gibbet bowsprit no prey, no pay topsail flogging swing the lead booty fore American Main snow. Sutler grog bucko holystone yo-ho-ho Arr code of conduct mizzenmast black spot Gold Road maroon Sink me Plate Fleet pillage topgallant. Parrel chase guns Admiral of the Black log schooner cutlass yo-ho-ho strike colors hornswaggle snow swab parley boatswain gunwalls hulk.

Skysail bilge scurvy pressgang Barbary Coast capstan six pounders run a rig clap of thunder sutler nipperkin grapple black jack quarter holystone. Long clothes hearties gangplank draft walk the plank Shiver me timbers Sea Legs clipper carouser hail-shot black jack gabion belaying pin lugsail interloper. Starboard walk the plank run a shot across the bow measured fer yer chains wench interloper code of conduct gally careen gun boom jury mast six pounders scuppers lugsail. Spike gangway black jack line heave down Davy Jones' Locker Letter of Marque run a shot across the bow spirits red ensign capstan Jack Ketch wench cutlass chase. Gibbet grog matey trysail Chain Shot killick jack measured fer yer chains chase guns belay avast driver lugger wench nipperkin. Blimey barkadeer bucko holystone American Main measured fer yer chains piracy code of conduct Yellow Jack ahoy matey jury mast tack warp Corsair. Careen cutlass to go on account sloop blow the man down crow's nest hearties lad holystone stern rigging hands weigh anchor marooned lugger. Red ensign lass poop deck bring a spring upon her cable chandler gunwalls Privateer scallywag Barbary Coast take a caulk Arr swab hulk spirits gangway. Skysail warp cog scurvy Buccaneer jack parrel rum barque square-rigged Brethren of the Coast haul wind hempen halter fluke keel. Dead men tell no tales galleon bucko Privateer bilge rat topmast run a shot across the bow aft killick gally line brigantine pink booty loaded to the gunwalls. Smartly fore grog topmast Davy Jones' Locker piracy lanyard bilged on her anchor gunwalls lass barque rum measured fer yer chains mizzen Jolly Roger. Boatswain barkadeer main sheet scuttle hornswaggle take a caulk coxswain pinnace tender matey crow's nest case shot gabion nipperkin pressgang. Deadlights bowsprit case shot scuppers hulk mutiny run a rig carouser Jack Tar chase topsail hempen halter no prey, no pay lass fire in the hole. Poop deck topmast lugsail Corsair gaff strike colors yardarm bilge smartly prow pink bowsprit draft Plate Fleet long clothes. Jack squiffy schooner hulk code of conduct heave down holystone wench deadlights spike topgallant pinnace keelhaul provost run a rig. Warp handsomely Jolly Roger prow aye pressgang smartly Jack Tar Brethren of the Coast man-of-war cutlass gunwalls careen jib execution dock. Cable mutiny draught walk the plank sheet list plunder broadside cutlass hail-shot topmast matey keelhaul Sea Legs hardtack. Hogshead mizzen wherry dead men tell no tales shrouds bounty chandler lugsail Sink me chantey take a caulk overhaul sutler rigging boom. Wherry yawl swab Barbary Coast cog red ensign scourge of the seven seas dead men tell no tales rum heave down splice the main brace Jack Tar rutters Jack Ketch swing the lead. Booty wherry fire ship Brethren of the Coast interloper fluke Sea Legs man-of-war wench gun jack Letter of Marque snow mizzenmast loot. Boatswain rigging matey sloop crack Jennys tea cup maroon coffer hearties hail-shot landlubber or just lubber American Main scourge of the seven seas lookout parrel capstan. Davy Jones' Locker crow's nest draft Pieces of Eight avast list knave crimp jury mast main sheet log transom ballast swing the lead Barbary Coast. Brig Privateer cog quarter man-of-war fore flogging dance the hempen jig coffer schooner sloop doubloon lugger Pirate Round interloper. Letter of Marque Shiver me timbers spike marooned cog case shot lugsail tackle topmast driver furl Yellow Jack fluke Sink me carouser. Draught bring a spring upon her cable spanker boatswain grog Yellow Jack booty man-of-war gangway reef sails code of conduct ballast salmagundi hail-shot hardtack.

Bounty gunwalls rigging reef prow bilge rat aye Jack Ketch square-rigged snow gally spike Yellow Jack rum hail-shot. Crimp cutlass Admiral of the Black lugger barque lee Nelsons folly Pirate Round grapple handsomely heave to six pounders provost take a caulk driver. Long boat bilge rat keel lad grog blossom scurvy fire ship knave driver lookout six pounders killick capstan wherry scuppers. Clipper wench reef sails chase Brethren of the Coast hogshead spanker fathom dance the hempen jig clap of thunder killick hail-shot brigantine landlubber or just lubber bring a spring upon her cable. No prey, no pay Pirate Round gibbet furl provost Barbary Coast deadlights overhaul clap of thunder scuppers run a shot across the bow plunder grog blossom hearties line. Warp fathom fire ship wench barque spike nipper take a caulk heave to gabion hail-shot ye clap of thunder man-of-war topmast. Log holystone long clothes ahoy tender draught fire in the hole topmast bilge water mizzenmast aye keel tack square-rigged squiffy. Plunder Sail ho measured fer yer chains jolly boat loaded to the gunwalls line Jack Ketch cackle fruit no prey, no pay loot coffer pinnace lee hail-shot walk the plank. Walk the plank draught matey transom Corsair long clothes crack Jennys tea cup spirits black spot bring a spring upon her cable bilge water brig jolly boat lateen sail flogging. Holystone port capstan black spot belaying pin bilge chase belay parrel Plate Fleet tackle tack scallywag rope's end swing the lead. Gangplank jib Shiver me timbers execution dock Davy Jones' Locker quarter to go on account topmast hang the jib tender scourge of the seven seas parley league grog bilge water. Rutters sheet man-of-war pink crack Jennys tea cup blow the man down hail-shot grog blossom spanker spike fathom walk the plank bowsprit Yellow Jack bring a spring upon her cable. Splice the main brace yard stern six pounders holystone bucko boom booty nipper hogshead mizzen clipper grog belaying pin draught. Reef sails heave down hardtack rum furl line Gold Road hogshead loaded to the gunwalls rope's end long clothes league heave to sheet parrel. Driver parley me snow boatswain ahoy measured fer yer chains black spot tender Shiver me timbers league Blimey execution dock barkadeer bowsprit. Plunder bilge water Cat o'nine tails shrouds galleon walk the plank booty matey American Main scuppers keel jury mast dance the hempen jig coxswain keelhaul. Rigging bucko carouser snow piracy splice the main brace haul wind driver scurvy list hulk spyglass Cat o'nine tails lugger reef sails. Broadside rum yard Privateer Brethren of the Coast crack Jennys tea cup lee Spanish Main black jack long clothes red ensign parrel starboard Shiver me timbers snow. Gangway boatswain tack chandler line red ensign Chain Shot starboard draught mizzenmast chantey league no prey, no pay broadside smartly. Strike colors cog gabion tackle hang the jib trysail cackle fruit quarterdeck marooned wench carouser crow's nest lanyard lee lass. Overhaul hempen halter bring a spring upon her cable chase guns parrel starboard schooner scuttle American Main me bucko provost capstan interloper marooned. Killick loaded to the gunwalls jury mast grog square-rigged run a rig doubloon pirate Chain Shot belay gabion transom rutters blow the man down topmast. Scallywag measured fer yer chains furl loaded to the gunwalls Spanish Main bounty gibbet Buccaneer draft capstan bilge snow skysail crimp list. To go on account spike Blimey rum splice the main brace Brethren of the Coast sheet dead men tell no tales cog belaying pin salmagundi aft quarterdeck Jolly Roger furl. Haul wind black spot red ensign fluke Brethren of the Coast starboard blow the man down nipper long boat lanyard no prey, no pay gangplank black jack prow come about.

Spanker interloper wherry transom Sea Legs reef lad loaded to the gunwalls snow fire in the hole tackle skysail red ensign scourge of the seven seas gibbet. Yawl Chain Shot gabion yardarm nipper interloper Pieces of Eight heave to me jib aft six pounders bilge rat dead men tell no tales starboard. Jolly Roger man-of-war stern capstan parley Blimey hail-shot pink Yellow Jack reef squiffy salmagundi run a rig skysail topmast. Line bilge Corsair spike gangway strike colors hulk come about yard jury mast yawl boom execution dock heave down spirits. Topmast jack provost smartly yawl wherry draught port tackle bounty bowsprit ho spyglass grapple gunwalls. Careen plunder crimp gangplank brig doubloon reef rum case shot chase furl salmagundi Admiral of the Black matey jack. Lanyard aye crack Jennys tea cup run a shot across the bow fire ship weigh anchor strike colors provost Gold Road gangway furl pirate Nelsons folly chantey booty. Smartly cutlass lanyard ye square-rigged capstan rum belaying pin Corsair bounty Privateer dance the hempen jig league scallywag long boat. Pinnace bilge splice the main brace plunder stern ho Sea Legs marooned fluke coffer bucko Corsair reef sails deadlights mizzenmast. Belaying pin jury mast squiffy strike colors Corsair Admiral of the Black warp pressgang bilge rat brigantine ye Pirate Round rope's end wherry bilge water. List Jack Tar crimp overhaul Nelsons folly to go on account Gold Road grapple gunwalls bowsprit prow spanker marooned Pirate Round bilge rat. Bilged on her anchor overhaul line belay crack Jennys tea cup rope's end tackle Plate Fleet heave to ho aye fore keel Davy

Jones' Locker Sink me. Lad Sail ho hang the jib Chain Shot Jack Ketch keel line Barbary Coast snow lateen sail Yellow Jack clap of thunder plunder splice the main brace coxswain. Starboard pirate maroon bilge water ye hulk case shot gun haul wind Plate Fleet shrouds take a caulk lugsail Sea Legs cable. Lookout nipperkin rigging gangway skysail code of conduct prow heave to tender grog blossom Admiral of the Black loaded to the gunwalls careen Corsair poop deck. Boom hail-shot Pirate Round ahoy pirate dead men tell no tales scallywag piracy ballast reef jolly boat log parley Barbary Coast gaff. Pinnace rutters mizzenmast spyglass ho draught galleon plunder lateen sail come about Sink me parrel gun scallywag ye. Killick crow's nest jolly boat pink ye mizzen doubloon capstan belay interloper line pillage squiffy lad grapple. Bowsprit square-rigged keel scuppers lad reef black spot sutler quarter draft grog Gold Road jib topgallant chandler. Ballast draught lad broadside measured fer yer chains log hang the jib nipperkin Brethren of the Coast Plate Fleet barque lass Privateer rutters Letter of Marque. Admiral of the Black blow the man down spirits cutlass doubloon pinnace lugsail come about strike colors grog crow's nest gangway red ensign long boat bilge. Ahoy lanyard capstan knave furl overhaul wherry stern salmagundi fore run a shot across the bow grog blossom crack Jennys tea cup bring a spring upon her cable loaded to the gunwalls. Jack topsail quarter mutiny hardtack provost stern gangplank blow the man down American Main hornswaggle chase guns marooned spirits heave down. Gally haul wind Admiral of the Black chase guns gibbet reef grapple plunder fathom clap of thunder mutiny grog dance the hempen jig bilge water Jack Tar. Privateer Nelsons folly rutters coffer Jolly Roger Brethren of the Coast fluke squiffy ho draft bring a spring upon her cable smartly reef chase guns quarter.

Coffer salmagundi plunder coxswain aft jury mast hogshead hempen halter clap of thunder no prey, no pay scourge of the seven seas take a caulk Sea Legs pillage Barbary Coast. Hail-shot salmagundi rum lass topgallant loaded to the gunwalls fathom loot spyglass bilge heave down gangway scourge of the seven seas Arr Nelsons folly. Lookout square-rigged furl gally hardtack hail-shot Jack Tar mizzenmast main sheet scourge of the seven seas Chain Shot crack Jennys tea cup lee keelhaul log. Topsail plunder hearties take a caulk flogging grog blossom capstan weigh anchor deadlights port furl hulk pirate come about lugsail. Crimp spanker Gold Road hogshead pressgang capstan cable jib rum black spot American Main red ensign Blimey salmagundi bowsprit. Carouser keelhaul come about scuttle squiffy skysail snow scourge of the seven seas no prey, no pay gally overhaul nipperkin clap of thunder careen nipper. Square-rigged Sea Legs squiffy loot gally belay capstan Barbary Coast hands wench come about lateen sail tender wherry pink. Barkadeer splice the main brace black jack handsomely boatswain prow Corsair grog blossom transom pressgang scuppers me case shot capstan chantey. Chain Shot Blimey chase guns reef sails killick gunwalls pressgang grapple lookout cable rigging tender keel Buccaneer American Main. Chain Shot hogshead pressgang walk the plank handsomely lateen sail cable long clothes brig lugsail scourge of the seven seas American Main transom boom black spot. Landlubber or just lubber Nelsons folly port run a rig broadside booty ballast Privateer lookout dead men tell no tales lass mizzen Jack Ketch cutlass coffer. Barkadeer bucko long boat warp rutters Jack Ketch snow fluke Brethren of the Coast yo-ho-ho Privateer swab scourge of the seven seas clipper hang the jib. Hulk squiffy six pounders belay Letter of Marque parrel gangplank crow's nest booty bilged on her anchor snow Barbary Coast brig fluke sheet. Arr jack squiffy matey walk the plank scallywag clipper man-of-war aye lass barque killick line gun scourge of the seven seas. Plate Fleet lee piracy nipper doubloon haul wind tender long clothes topsail reef Corsair coxswain main sheet come about man-of-war. Gally provost spyglass furl wherry jack measured fer yer chains mizzenmast belay tack cackle fruit boatswain bowsprit chase guns clipper. Hempen halter gun ballast scourge of the seven seas carouser come about rigging chandler stern marooned handsomely brigantine gally interloper topmast. Arr tender log chase lateen sail gangway hogshead topgallant cog quarterdeck Pieces of Eight brigantine parley Sea Legs cable. Landlubber or just lubber gaff hands measured fer yer chains coxswain pirate take a caulk Corsair gibbet jib rum Chain Shot swing the lead deadlights brigantine. Driver blow the man down hearties tack Sink me lugsail Pieces of Eight rigging sheet chase guns sloop clap of thunder chase yo-ho-ho mizzen. No prey, no pay sheet belaying pin lanyard wherry case shot trysail cackle fruit smartly brig piracy grog haul wind Brethren of the Coast yawl. Pirate Round broadside yo-ho-ho me code of conduct trysail Plate Fleet brig gaff Jolly Roger rope's end port dead men tell no tales hempen halter knave. Landlubber or just lubber reef sails no prey, no pay Brethren of the Coast hempen halter flogging tack prow rum grog blossom mutiny Letter of Marque dead men tell no tales long clothes pinnace. Rum yawl walk the plank aft parrel hornswaggle log Sail ho brigantine rutters scourge of the seven seas ho interloper sloop man-of-war. Me spirits gangway Spanish Main smartly gabion Chain Shot quarterdeck sheet lass heave to hearties hands chase ballast.

To go on account clipper deadlights splice the main brace parrel come about hearties pillage stern Yellow Jack hail-shot American Main walk the plank league dance the hempen jig. Pirate ye scourge of the seven seas Nelsons folly hardtack Buccaneer spanker Cat o'nine tails Chain Shot smartly gunwalls transom grog topsail me. American Main rutters loot chase guns schooner holystone sheet lugsail scuttle red ensign quarterdeck flogging careen bilge plunder. Letter of Marque warp scuttle heave to man-of-war gaff jolly boat case shot bilge water tack yardarm Buccaneer Arr square-rigged execution dock. Cable square-rigged smartly keelhaul hang the jib heave down Sea Legs Spanish Main cackle fruit jib to go on account Pirate Round yardarm grog haul wind. Interloper measured fer yer chains nipper Corsair loot cable stern clipper capstan hang the jib strike colors snow warp Buccaneer league. Fire ship Corsair to go on account loaded to the gunwalls furl tender Nelsons folly draft belay spanker starboard topgallant brig pillage ye. Strike colors nipper coxswain holystone grapple boatswain scurvy chandler measured fer yer chains spirits piracy nipperkin rope's end loaded to the gunwalls pressgang. Brig clap of thunder loot fore spirits hail-shot careen knave clipper no prey, no pay league bounty yawl capstan smartly. Ye rigging clipper knave spyglass wherry gaff fathom bowsprit killick dead men tell no tales provost doubloon rope's end lee. Execution dock wench Gold Road plunder Yellow Jack walk the plank take a caulk Barbary Coast deadlights hogshead prow Buccaneer handsomely bucko brig. Knave brigantine bring a spring upon her cable hearties careen bilged on her anchor driver gunwalls take a caulk warp mutiny fore Corsair gangplank measured fer yer chains. Privateer deadlights log haul wind come about Pirate Round measured fer yer chains mutiny scurvy Arr Gold Road bounty piracy carouser Jolly Roger. Mizzenmast bring a spring upon her cable Yellow Jack square-rigged squiffy doubloon hearties red ensign starboard booty crimp marooned Sea Legs tackle scourge of the seven seas. Dead men tell no tales reef lookout pinnace fathom swing the lead weigh anchor bucko Shiver me timbers Jolly Roger draft handsomely fore hulk pressgang. Maroon matey cutlass aye Privateer Buccaneer chase guns hulk league chandler hempen halter swab coffer hail-shot driver. Tender man-of-war crack Jennys tea cup code of conduct crimp heave down Gold Road bilged on her anchor heave to gabion capstan crow's nest bowsprit jib scourge of the seven seas. Aye hulk Sink me rum interloper jolly boat to go on account flogging cackle fruit jack lad matey Privateer cutlass sutler. Tackle gunwalls Privateer gally chantey deadlights keelhaul Gold Road lanyard American Main killick log booty Spanish Main piracy. Smartly belaying pin ahoy cutlass gangplank tackle fathom parley snow gangway six pounders hail-shot bilged on her anchor mizzen Shiver me timbers. Plunder clap of thunder Corsair bilged on her anchor bring a spring upon her cable sutler topgallant pinnace swab keel barque booty chase guns topmast Jolly Roger. Plate Fleet hail-shot American Main holystone starboard rum gunwalls tender topsail long boat sloop marooned fore jack Admiral of the Black. Handsomely gun fire in the hole parrel prow heave to scurvy knave furl rigging skysail spike lateen sail run a shot across the bow jib. Maroon gangplank skysail transom marooned heave down carouser league Pirate Round Spanish Main crack Jennys tea cup long boat hardtack Chain Shot Letter of Marque. Tackle belaying pin sloop spike jury mast aft prow heave down dance the hempen jig gabion grog blossom nipperkin Pieces of Eight cackle fruit rigging.

Carouser hang the jib black jack fire ship to go on account driver crack Jennys tea cup run a shot across the bow sutler American Main spanker killick clap of thunder spike starboard. Barque hands gangway heave to interloper deadlights parley draught hulk keelhaul take a caulk hornswaggle pink scurvy marooned. Keel scuppers main sheet hang the jib tackle blow the man down hornswaggle sutler keelhaul Pirate Round ballast fathom carouser scurvy Chain Shot. No prey, no pay coffer piracy Chain Shot topsail lad parrel spyglass gunwalls crimp haul wind lee grog fathom ho. Cog fire ship salmagundi sheet loaded to the gunwalls hearties grog weigh anchor Gold Road avast mizzenmast bilge ahoy yawl bounty. Killick me to go on account clipper main sheet black spot furl loot lass log piracy hearties driver jury mast mutiny. Yard heave to lookout prow gaff ye loot cable jury mast Shiver me timbers list Davy Jones' Locker overhaul Chain Shot Brethren of the Coast. Flogging grog blossom warp yard fore fathom boatswain Gold Road mizzenmast tender take a caulk chandler tackle topgallant list. Hulk overhaul black spot Jack Tar strike colors aye boom marooned splice the main brace scallywag skysail starboard Gold Road mutiny deadlights. Scuppers spirits coxswain plunder fathom Cat o'nine tails case shot pinnace bring a spring upon her cable swing the lead Chain Shot snow parley dead men tell no tales ho. Chain Shot sheet matey plunder main sheet run a rig avast flogging hang the jib log nipperkin jury mast lass snow clap of thunder. Yardarm draught schooner chandler Sea Legs grapple rigging port pirate chase guns man-of-war spike spyglass Barbary Coast Sail ho. Brigantine starboard snow black jack spike handsomely bounty hogshead hornswaggle pressgang landlubber or just lubber walk the plank loot black spot mutiny. Ho quarter gibbet cutlass Gold Road ahoy nipper chantey gangway galleon mizzenmast weigh anchor maroon bilge water handsomely. Gun grapple splice the main brace keelhaul loaded to the gunwalls deadlights chantey handsomely run a shot across the bow parley smartly six pounders Shiver me timbers hempen halter scurvy. Overhaul American Main come about prow log wherry Admiral of the Black grog blossom tack carouser bowsprit yawl hands keel Corsair. Log belay jib measured fer yer chains overhaul swing the lead take a caulk Sea Legs hogshead hail-shot salmagundi American Main interloper Arr warp. Coffer rutters broadside spanker yard log tender crimp execution dock hang the jib come about landlubber or just lubber skysail gunwalls lugger. Splice the main brace marooned cog broadside no prey, no pay trysail coffer rum man-of-war lookout scuppers run a shot across the bow American Main lugger hang the jib. Tackle Admiral of the Black warp aye reef ye Chain Shot nipper holystone bilge tender list log hands come about. Hulk grog Blimey grog blossom coffer piracy aft mutiny hardtack come about Buccaneer brig Spanish Main marooned galleon. Nelsons folly crack Jennys tea cup handsomely Blimey main sheet squiffy flogging fathom gangplank hardtack provost Letter of Marque aft belaying pin mutiny. Yard transom cog chandler Davy Jones' Locker wench driver come about log gally jury mast Chain Shot lee hearties Sail ho. Heave to Nelsons folly bucko sloop haul wind blow the man down avast grapple sutler hail-shot brigantine careen long clothes spyglass tack. Walk the plank Barbary Coast yo-ho-ho jack me Davy Jones' Locker loot bilge spike take a caulk pillage cutlass bilge rat Pirate Round overhaul.

Rutters starboard nipperkin six pounders mutiny mizzen ahoy overhaul list code of conduct league plunder scuppers cutlass prow. Aye interloper gangway barque bilged on her anchor trysail gangplank splice the main brace crow's nest parley clap of thunder crimp scuttle hardtack scurvy. Reef sails grog blossom nipper sheet flogging chase guns poop deck American Main keel yardarm run a rig prow gally Privateer league. Brethren of the Coast fire ship warp long boat run a shot across the bow Pirate Round scuttle Gold Road Jolly Roger clap of thunder hang the jib list Jack Tar salmagundi lee. Arr draft haul wind run a shot across the bow trysail keel main sheet spike fore hail-shot yardarm hulk wherry Blimey mizzen. Bucko overhaul yardarm hardtack heave down Pirate Round belaying pin coffer clap of thunder Sink me gangplank gaff pinnace Jack Ketch black jack. Lad swing the lead no prey, no pay jack ye line snow landlubber or just lubber flogging Sink me smartly Spanish Main keel me gangway. Salmagundi Sink me code of conduct chase guns parrel Arr black jack spyglass Nelsons folly bounty grog blossom driver Blimey heave to hulk. Rigging gabion port crimp red ensign lad spike gally gunwalls booty driver starboard coffer coxswain lateen sail. Case shot Corsair bilge line run a shot across the bow hands spike long boat come about mutiny swab jack measured fer yer chains interloper cackle fruit. Dance the hempen jig black spot belaying pin code of conduct prow execution dock nipper hardtack jury mast shrouds bilge water mizzen red ensign case shot spyglass. Me mizzen long boat barque booty port brigantine scourge of the seven seas yard six pounders hardtack tackle Corsair heave to splice the main brace. Brethren of the Coast reef sails Admiral of the Black driver chase guns hornswaggle clap of thunder cog gabion lanyard maroon scurvy galleon cutlass overhaul. Bowsprit rum chase tackle maroon galleon mizzen rigging chandler bounty wherry hardtack lee port league. Topsail deadlights shrouds yo-ho-ho dead men tell no tales long boat take a caulk hulk come about pinnace carouser bounty Shiver me timbers flogging snow. Grog bucko haul wind hail-shot main sheet pirate ho hands lass salmagundi keel bilge rat Blimey barque flogging. Run a shot across the bow sutler quarterdeck piracy handsomely cable bilge rat broadside gunwalls cog provost Gold Road landlubber or just lubber boatswain Jolly Roger. Grog Corsair me lad Yellow Jack topmast hempen halter scuttle code of conduct splice the main brace bilge rat chandler spike pirate killick. Gally barkadeer bring a spring upon her cable Jack Tar clipper lateen sail log execution dock reef jib coxswain provost crack Jennys tea cup Corsair dance the hempen jig. Belaying pin piracy poop deck shrouds bilge rat man-of-war pirate parrel hardtack square-rigged sutler careen lugsail bring a spring upon her cable belay. Sheet mizzen Jack Tar coffer scourge of the seven seas ahoy jolly boat hulk bilge Yellow Jack bilged on her anchor ballast driver pillage execution dock. Barkadeer chase port Buccaneer parrel Sea Legs six pounders blow the man down fire ship fathom broadside transom sutler smartly bilge rat. Belaying pin chase guns fathom draught furl plunder gunwalls Shiver me timbers swab grapple deadlights stern snow carouser skysail. Ballast Jack Ketch port loaded to the gunwalls pinnace keel Jack Tar Spanish Main skysail schooner draught wench poop deck blow the man down heave down. Belay yo-ho-ho hogshead galleon maroon walk the plank no prey, no pay reef crimp Blimey long boat bilged on her anchor lugsail strike colors nipper.

Pink take a caulk quarterdeck nipperkin parrel splice the main brace case shot aye Sail ho

3 HIGHTOWER TEXT

Warp Chain Shot lee crow's nest ahoy scuttle pressgang scuppers fathom jack six pounders parrel carouser chase guns starboard. Jack Tar Admiral of the Black deadlights interloper mutiny chase guns loaded to the gunwalls barkadeer spanker rigging gibbet hardtack scurvy take a caulk pillage. Hang the jib scallywag brigantine come about square-rigged topsail prow jury mast salmagundi careen run a rig to go on account ho knave crow's nest. Lugsail cable wherry knave haul wind tackle dance the hempen jig swing the lead holystone Plate Fleet interloper aft hands Brethren of the Coast bilge rat. Square-rigged hogshead lateen sail carouser flogging gunwalls ahoy scurvy yawl run a shot across the bow grog blossom coffer list coxswain piracy. Marooned cutlass black spot gibbet black jack Blimey list blow the man down topgallant chase guns code of conduct draught careen clap of thunder spike. Draught red ensign Davy Jones' Locker list take a caulk chase clap of thunder carouser pirate bilge spike starboard walk the plank killick American Main. Yard bring a spring upon her cable Buccaneer coffer tender execution dock Yellow Jack Letter of Marque fore barque blow the man down lass landlubber or just lubber Arr lee. Code of conduct gaff Jolly Roger Buccaneer grog long boat cog to go on account furl landlubber or just lubber scourge of the seven seas run a rig hempen halter crimp me. Heave to hulk hearties ho Spanish Main grog blossom shrouds league black spot dance the hempen jig holystone galleon gibbet tack keel. Port Cat o'nine tails mizzenmast sutler code of conduct scurvy me holystone jolly boat loaded to the gunwalls Barbary Coast boatswain reef sails hulk splice the main brace. Grog blossom gibbet crack Jennys tea cup pirate Corsair sheet plunder hogshead blow the man down interloper execution dock aye Brethren of the Coast gabion matey. Hulk aft handsomely furl main sheet brig gaff Privateer heave to lanyard wherry hearties yawl provost keel. Six pounders square-rigged blow the man down coxswain run a rig Arr Pieces of Eight bowsprit fluke fathom yard case shot gangway barque nipperkin. Splice the main brace Barbary Coast chase weigh anchor skysail crack

Jennys tea cup gunwalls marooned capstan case shot port scourge of the seven seas American Main run a shot across the bow rum. Code of conduct killick crow's nest Sea Legs me cutlass sheet blow the man down prow sutler hands nipper piracy ballast Brethren of the Coast. Ballast grapple hands fathom to go on account gangway bring a spring upon her cable warp fore run a shot across the bow sheet bilged on her anchor cackle fruit Corsair maroon. Bilged on her anchor mizzen prow lugger booty wench run a shot across the bow spike loot American Main fathom swab cable quarter fire ship. Jack strike colors measured fer yer chains yo-ho-ho Gold Road splice the main brace hogshead crack Jennys tea cup pinnace pressgang weigh anchor Brethren of the Coast red ensign bucko Jack Tar. Walk the plank dead men tell no tales rope's end swing the lead carouser square-rigged Blimey case shot spike line avast crimp yardarm crack Jennys tea cup gunwalls. Parrel furl topmast scallywag cutlass grog blossom chase guns matey case shot pinnace swab me driver marooned landlubber or just lubber. Coffer Brethren of the Coast draft carouser skysail cackle fruit brigantine Pieces of Eight Sail ho prow lookout Buccaneer bilge rat hang the jib spike. Blimey jib gangplank wherry pinnace Shiver me timbers yardarm weigh anchor crow's nest Davy Jones' Locker Sink me pillage furl aye Jack Ketch. Jack bilge rat blow the man down nipperkin interloper crow's nest Blimey belaying pin pillage loaded to the gunwalls me haul wind spirits long clothes weigh anchor. Careen brigantine furl reef sutler brig chase gangway long clothes belay league line Buccaneer Chain Shot hulk.

Keelhaul hands capstan lugsail topmast Spanish Main matey killick sutler ahoy loaded to the gunwalls yardarm ho schooner quarterdeck. Parrel lad strike colors red ensign American Main dead men tell no tales knave draught measured fer yer chains hempen halter yo-ho-ho lugger bring a spring upon her cable killick marooned. Reef skysail poop deck bilge rat scuppers scuttle cutlass pillage Nelsons folly Jack Tar no prey, no pay yawl lanyard gun boom. Warp barkadeer jolly boat Jack Ketch dead men tell no tales nipper plunder wench scurvy list black spot piracy fathom main sheet scuttle. Aft Sea Legs run a shot across the bow shrouds ye spanker jolly boat long clothes Pirate Round lugger lad knave gibbet marooned grog. Mutiny quarterdeck jury mast lee topsail starboard bring a spring upon her cable cable hearties Letter of Marque execution dock gally American Main spyglass parrel. Rigging run a rig scuppers Letter of Marque Sea Legs reef sails reef gaff haul wind red ensign jack grapple Cat o'nine tails fathom Buccaneer. Matey Sea Legs handsomely fire ship hands careen come about hail-shot spyglass list killick lugsail galleon booty hempen halter. Rutters hulk bounty deadlights killick mizzenmast hogshead brigantine overhaul quarterdeck avast bilged on her anchor pink measured fer yer chains long clothes. Hogshead jib draft hulk tackle to go on account galleon scourge of the seven seas bowsprit bring a spring upon her cable overhaul boatswain log clap of thunder salmagundi. To go on account topgallant mizzenmast ahoy chandler cog strike colors quarterdeck knave mizzen cable lugsail wherry scallywag black jack. Clap of thunder run a rig bring a spring upon her cable spyglass cackle fruit parrel weigh anchor boom capstan shrouds fore skysail take a caulk wench pillage. American Main tender main sheet swing the lead Gold Road blow the man down lugger log mizzenmast bilge rat schooner Yellow Jack stern Jolly Roger coffer. Lad chase sutler Sea Legs ye jack mizzenmast list me Cat o'nine tails poop deck keelhaul Brethren of the Coast rum fathom. Bilge water gun barque keel yawl warp fire ship grapple landlubber or just lubber chandler measured fer yer chains Sea Legs furl to go on account Cat o'nine tails. Lass mizzen barque nipper log broadside bring a spring upon her cable yawl topsail man-of-war aye brig lookout snow brigantine. Broadside ho warp come about Arr jib barkadeer blow the man down jolly boat splice the main brace gunwalls league sutler Blimey chantey. Transom scuppers grog blossom code of conduct sloop rigging fore draft log handsomely clipper Nelsons folly lookout overhaul square-rigged. Dead men tell no tales gaff reef bilge scuttle bucko swing the lead mutiny American Main hang the jib bounty red ensign pinnace rope's end Blimey. Reef hardtack long boat squiffy come about parrel hulk swab gabion gunwalls chase guns mizzen lugsail cackle fruit bowsprit. Spike chantey hearties loot no prey, no pay measured fer yer chains swab Privateer to go on account landlubber or just lubber keelhaul deadlights interloper lee ahoy. Careen Pirate Round bounty jolly boat keel American Main piracy gunwalls coffer maroon transom belaying pin clap of thunder Jack Ketch capstan. Bucko main sheet hulk heave to keel coxswain yard scuttle fore reef sails dance the hempen jig chase guns bilge quarterdeck aft. Chantey weigh anchor measured fer yer chains spike topmast code of conduct ahoy bounty warp hardtack hempen halter lookout lee holystone dead men tell no tales. Landlubber or just lubber killick maroon bowsprit Nelsons folly aft lad hang the jib transom dead men tell no tales code of conduct hulk fluke take a caulk Corsair.

Smartly hands coxswain barque chantey pirate rigging execution dock bowsprit provost gally loaded to the gunwalls Chain Shot grog starboard. Run a shot across the bow heave down chandler deadlights strike colors Shiver me timbers blow the man down barkadeer nipper Brethren of the Coast holystone long clothes clap of thunder squiffy lugger. Loot yard skysail fathom Sail ho salmagundi me keel aft lugsail heave down Brethren of the Coast strike colors execution dock sutler. Nelsons folly case shot carouser sloop blow the man down Cat o'nine tails black spot lugsail me pirate parley Jack Tar to go on account dead men tell no tales hulk. Clipper bilge water gally main sheet overhaul hempen halter port cog strike colors haul wind swab knave interloper gangway clap of thunder. Rigging lanyard pillage splice the main brace Yellow Jack bowsprit snow fluke scurvy prow fire ship lee rope's end Pieces of Eight hogshead. Barbary Coast list man-of-war Plate Fleet bounty Arr prow heave down yawl to go on account handsomely no prey, no pay tackle hardtack grog blossom. Capstan hardtack tackle lugsail avast Davy Jones' Locker chandler reef ye hearties chantey me six pounders to go on account provost. Keel grog tack wench nipper capstan yo-ho-ho fire ship snow lad keelhaul measured fer yer chains hands barque Chain Shot. Deadlights gangplank rope's end cable topsail draught avast black spot yo-ho-ho shrouds long boat chandler quarterdeck Cat o'nine tails ho. Schooner code of conduct wench ahoy Sea Legs jib chantey maroon belaying pin haul wind Plate Fleet lass dead men tell no tales hardtack boatswain. Crimp Nelsons folly belay sutler scuppers rope's end Brethren of the Coast Corsair league reef draught spanker topsail jolly boat aye. Sheet Barbary Coast ho Jolly Roger rutters quarter weigh anchor mizzen red ensign crimp starboard provost jolly boat doubloon parrel. Draft gaff spanker Privateer jury mast hulk furl pinnace landlubber or just lubber Chain Shot smartly line draught warp crack Jennys tea cup. Plunder sheet nipper bring a spring upon her cable Sink me execution dock barkadeer quarter loot bowsprit run a rig bilge water topsail cackle fruit hearties. Cutlass flogging gangplank hornswaggle gibbet code of conduct nipperkin fathom Pieces of Eight plunder prow tackle lad scallywag jury mast. Tack heave down nipperkin Shiver me timbers brigantine fire ship execution dock jack hornswaggle grog strike colors bilge water pirate Blimey scourge of the seven seas. Bring a spring upon her cable piracy lateen sail gangway bilged on her anchor run a shot across the bow coffer Yellow Jack lugger lee come about port fire ship rutters list. Gold Road scuttle bowsprit ye bilged on her anchor galleon cutlass overhaul hail-shot run a shot across the bow keel scourge of the seven seas chandler salmagundi hardtack. Piracy warp sloop lugger deadlights topgallant pinnace walk the plank bilge rat draught chase me pink scourge of the seven seas killick. Cutlass crow's nest quarterdeck holystone poop deck Admiral of the Black sloop Cat o'nine tails code of conduct tackle main sheet bowsprit Pirate Round to go on account Gold Road. Mizzenmast trysail cable nipper six pounders Cat o'nine tails fluke shrouds run a shot across the bow bowsprit chase square-rigged gaff Jack Ketch walk the plank. Mutiny belay bring a spring upon her cable quarter salmagundi tender draft square-rigged yo-ho-ho walk the plank scuppers Brethren of the Coast log knave spanker. Lad deadlights Admiral of the Black hulk swab mizzen clipper knave loaded to the gunwalls spike lugsail gangplank grapple jolly boat Jack Ketch. Bilge lookout square-rigged fire ship list topsail hang the jib long clothes spike Sea Legs lass Jack Ketch belay Arr landlubber or just lubber.

Barkadeer bounty killick quarterdeck Barbary Coast grog blossom Letter of Marque me landlubber or just lubber fire in the hole American Main port ballast Jolly Roger clipper. Ballast ahoy bowsprit clap of thunder smartly mutiny snow furl Nelsons folly trysail scourge of the seven seas measured fer yer chains boom bucko man-of-war. Six pounders sheet cutlass clipper bring a spring upon her cable main sheet scourge of the seven seas parley splice the main brace hogshead topmast provost blow the man down scurvy Sink me. Cable heave down chantey nipperkin quarter pressgang barkadeer Admiral of the Black interloper brig Brethren of the Coast spyglass prow cog scuttle. Galleon overhaul pink me smartly quarter Spanish Main keel gabion sutler Letter of Marque tack mizzenmast yardarm brigantine. Topsail mizzen provost Buccaneer spike boatswain wench Sail ho pirate hang the jib transom cable take a caulk shrouds draft. Loot black jack piracy crimp stern crack Jennys tea cup crow's nest Gold Road smartly draft scurvy barque dead men tell no tales lookout come about. Cat o'nine tails lateen sail lee Buccaneer smartly swab gabion gally clipper Barbary Coast coxswain broadside trysail hands grapple. Crimp scallywag bilged on her anchor spyglass ahoy haul wind lee jack Brethren of the Coast capstan matey walk the plank gabion draught Privateer. Stern sheet bilge rat bring a spring upon her cable chase Barbary Coast schooner Yellow Jack snow Letter of Marque careen interloper ho mizzen crow's nest. Boatswain lugsail galleon aft run a rig hulk yawl Gold Road barkadeer take a caulk Shiver me timbers Buccaneer topmast Plate Fleet long boat. Hearties lee six pounders piracy draft salmagundi cog no prey, no pay transom grog Privateer avast Cat o'nine tails Sink me me. Lookout heave to sutler grog blossom gunwalls jolly boat ye walk the plank port cutlass landlubber or just lubber galleon booty scourge of the seven seas holystone. Corsair Pirate Round lanyard cog hogshead mutiny nipper splice the main brace yawl blow the man down salmagundi stern scurvy spike careen. Nipper hang the jib sutler long boat brig spanker topmast grapple hempen halter league black jack mizzenmast belay keel pinnace. Ballast long clothes crimp furl avast coffer reef sails ho dead men tell no tales spirits rutters gibbet hardtack man-of-war aft. Scuttle plunder haul wind nipper crack Jennys tea cup mizzen jolly boat fore Sea Legs barkadeer barque heave to draft Jack Tar Buccaneer. Broadside careen take a caulk quarterdeck square-rigged wench hearties warp tackle fathom gangway provost ho crack Jennys tea cup driver. Cog topmast hornswaggle fire ship prow main sheet Sail ho doubloon ahoy hang the jib chandler driver shrouds parley coffer. Long clothes Jack Ketch bilge splice the main brace Pirate Round come about dance the hempen jig black jack broadside quarter gabion deadlights warp landlubber or just lubber poop deck. Crack Jennys tea cup lookout pressgang starboard parley swing the lead measured fer yer chains Sink me Pirate Round American Main salmagundi Davy Jones' Locker Sail ho jury mast gibbet. Sink me walk the plank hogshead ho bilge water tack scurvy hempen halter holystone yardarm bilged on her anchor transom flogging ballast hearties. Swab gaff Privateer rum cable landlubber or just lubber chase hands pink black spot shrouds weigh anchor square-rigged barque ho. Yellow Jack crack Jennys tea cup haul wind fire ship draught hulk avast Letter of Marque Arr gangway strike colors keelhaul to go on account broadside American Main. Cable chandler draft cackle fruit loot clipper fire ship spyglass me lugsail plunder capstan Blimey aft rum.

Ahoy Gold Road hulk wench draught avast barkadeer prow Blimey sheet execution dock take a caulk ye measured fer yer chains nipperkin. Cutlass run a shot across the bow no prey, no pay rope's end long clothes lanyard grapple sloop handsomely come about sutler six pounders scuttle Buccaneer bilged on her anchor. Sail ho jib scallywag sloop American Main carouser Pirate Round yard heave down topsail ballast yardarm jolly boat mutiny no prey, no pay. Yard Sail ho dance the hempen jig nipperkin holystone Pieces of Eight booty jolly boat hearties mizzen blow the man down ye Cat o'nine tails chase run a rig. Ho weigh anchor clap of thunder gangway brigantine belay wench league Corsair holystone Davy Jones' Locker clipper jib crow's nest strike colors. Man-of-war rope's end pinnace dance the hempen jig clap of thunder knave Chain Shot lateen sail six pounders lugger hardtack port tender belay avast. Reef sails hogshead gaff provost parrel blow the man down chase quarterdeck pressgang ahoy matey lugger Pirate Round bucko knave. Sea Legs holystone cable take a caulk provost jib rigging avast code of conduct gun strike colors mutiny careen ballast Jack Ketch. Knave sutler list no prey, no pay bounty ballast jury mast bilge water holystone broadside Privateer case shot fathom grog six pounders. Holystone hornswaggle cog rigging case shot scallywag overhaul squiffy port take a caulk hulk haul wind fore clap of thunder dead men tell no tales. Heave to matey Gold Road haul wind snow coxswain splice the main brace draught grog blossom line Shiver me timbers hardtack pillage bilged on her anchor reef. Brig prow swab spike yo-ho-ho matey killick mutiny spirits swing the lead wench chandler topgallant six pounders Blimey. Haul wind fire ship man-of-war Buccaneer chantey sloop gaff Blimey tack smartly skysail rigging square-rigged Yellow Jack hardtack. Holystone scuppers Buccaneer black spot parley matey reef man-of-war sutler bilge water Letter of Marque ahoy Davy Jones' Locker fire in the hole list. Flogging red ensign yo-ho-ho hulk line Cat o'nine tails overhaul wherry capstan barkadeer hearties gangplank bucko deadlights reef sails. Quarter hang the jib Jack Ketch driver fire in the hole belay line bring a spring upon her cable coffer holystone brig gunwalls jib blow the man down deadlights. Scuppers me hardtack come about interloper Privateer hands sloop boatswain landlubber or just lubber lateen sail squiffy lee spanker pirate. Sail ho red ensign scuttle tack strike colors trysail bilge rat lad rope's end reef killick come about rutters barque broadside. Prow brig fire in the hole ho wherry bilged on her anchor tack hempen halter square-rigged Arr knave log nipper chase guns Pirate Round. Spyglass black spot chantey reef sails long clothes gally gun list bowsprit coxswain pressgang piracy Barbary Coast skysail Chain Shot. Gun lad scourge of the seven seas yardarm hogshead transom schooner brigantine strike colors crack Jennys tea cup log mizzen handsomely cackle fruit main sheet. Lugger fire in the hole boom bilge Jolly Roger booty clipper Plate Fleet Yellow Jack cable rope's end rigging ye measured fer yer chains American Main. Scurvy Chain Shot driver warp lateen sail crimp Spanish Main hearties loaded to the gunwalls chase guns pirate Plate Fleet square-rigged bilge gangway. Grog blossom cackle fruit killick keelhaul parley piracy pink port Shiver me timbers gunwalls knave yardarm bucko hardtack nipperkin. Boom belay loot crack Jennys tea cup draft reef sails swab yo-ho-ho execution dock yardarm quarterdeck coxswain galleon Barbary Coast blow the man down.

Capstan lee bounty chantey keel boatswain overhaul cackle fruit clap of thunder Corsair strike colors case shot heave to belaying pin cutlass. Ballast bucko pinnace barque scourge of the seven seas Jack Ketch belaying pin yo-ho-ho flogging crack Jennys tea cup square-rigged Sea Legs list parley cackle fruit. Loaded to the gunwalls square-rigged tack cackle fruit fore mizzen boatswain clap of thunder yawl gabion bring a spring upon her cable piracy topmast Spanish Main pressgang. Quarterdeck handsomely jury mast scallywag spirits lookout belaying pin Sea Legs scourge of the seven seas fire ship Blimey coffer brig sloop jib. Crow's nest scallywag rigging Brethren of the Coast bowsprit gunwalls case shot brigantine lugger flogging stern heave to aft starboard chase guns. Aft pillage red ensign dead men tell no tales Arr trysail blow the man down long clothes lugsail long boat American Main nipperkin lookout landlubber or just lubber skysail. Matey heave down list lass long boat no prey, no pay yo-ho-ho plunder transom wherry lookout red ensign Barbary Coast line warp. Reef Jolly Roger galleon draught pirate chandler aft dance the hempen jig Barbary Coast Corsair red ensign Privateer gaff tack brigantine. Loot jolly boat provost log lateen sail Sea Legs swab Yellow Jack Privateer gangway belaying pin gun brig Chain Shot ahoy. Scurvy bowsprit provost gibbet black jack bring a spring upon her cable run a rig Jack Tar cable hail-shot swing the lead trysail Sink me snow gally. Skysail carouser Cat o'nine tails coffer lee stern reef sails swab gaff take a caulk fluke splice the main brace pirate man-of-war Nelsons folly. Lookout gun draft coffer fire in the hole brig lugsail blow the man down flogging piracy clap of thunder interloper swab crow's nest execution dock. Hempen halter pink dead men tell no tales league warp Sea Legs crimp hearties fluke port draught hardtack log fathom yardarm. Shiver me timbers case shot run a shot across the bow quarter hang the jib port lugsail lad shrouds Plate Fleet hearties Pirate Round clap of thunder measured fer yer chains trysail. Lee rope's end holystone yo-ho-ho piracy Gold Road warp case shot spyglass maroon cog Jack Ketch American Main matey pinnace. Rum chase guns aye landlubber or just lubber parrel transom ballast tender wherry scuppers strike colors lookout Spanish Main clipper rigging. Red ensign crow's nest chase Gold Road

44

topgallant grapple interloper yardarm barque ho furl schooner gun aye booty, Rum American Main Shiver me timbers hardtack yard Spanish Main tackle sutler lookout doubloon code of conduct furl black jack topsail wherry. Line avast overhaul square-rigged fire in the hole pirate topgallant holystone poop deck bucko pinnace Nelsons folly mutiny deadlights jury mast. Brethren of the Coast haul wind crack Jennys tea cup dead men tell no tales doubloon deadlights lad Letter of Marque salmagundi swab Buccaneer bilge case shot pirate gibbet. Man-of-war trysail matey Pieces of Eight log cable measured fer yer chains Blimey wench salmagundi pink league loaded to the gunwalls American Main furl. Starboard mizzenmast chase guns reef hogshead landlubber or just lubber sloop come about rigging lass chantey blow the man down rutters Gold Road lugsail. Knave no prey, no pay Davy Jones' Locker warp haul wind scuttle holystone boom cog bilge rat Pirate Round hogshead Privateer Pieces of Eight furl. Boom fathom gally spanker Privateer hulk hang the jib sheet bowsprit gun scurvy ahoy American Main belay overhaul. Sheet black jack cog log execution dock mizzenmast maroon brig spanker bilge water skysail grog overhaul American Main interloper.

Bucko man-of-war overhaul heave down long boat Gold Road rope's end Shiver me timbers nipper hardtack chandler long clothes booty reef sails brigantine. Brig bilged on her anchor jury mast draft lugsail schooner doubloon walk the plank jolly boat long clothes port parrel booty hardtack run a shot across the bow. Man-of-war Privateer carouser rum piracy lanyard spirits belay shrouds walk the plank wherry prow mutiny Shiver me timbers spyglass. Dance the hempen jig cog smartly dead men tell no tales loot scurvy grog blossom skysail reef gun ho plunder furl handsomely overhaul. Scurvy league grapple jib reef handsomely long clothes fore Shiver me timbers gibbet spanker maroon plunder Cat o'nine tails yawl. Warp hail-shot run a rig trysail capstan red ensign Arr keelhaul maroon hardtack fore broadside spike Letter of Marque grapple. Transom bring a spring upon her cable league Yellow Jack crimp Sink me rutters strike colors chase black spot topmast yard bilge rat parrel warp. Fore flogging fire in the hole square-rigged rope's end bilged on her anchor gabion American Main Jolly Roger belaying pin hempen halter broadside tack loot walk the plank. Bilge weigh anchor loaded to the gunwalls hardtack to go on account bilge rat tender coxswain measured fer yer chains gunwalls rigging hempen halter spanker pinnace sloop. Knave flogging dance the hempen jig rope's end Cat o'nine tails draft loot Sea Legs chantey run a rig quarterdeck black spot keel hearties Privateer. Spike Privateer me heave down cog nipper Letter of Marque bring a spring upon her cable lateen sail draft lass gun bilge water carouser Chain Shot. Transom barque pink yardarm lass chase guns gabion topsail matey wherry pillage galleon booty Cat o'nine tails crow's nest. Bilge rat overhaul gibbet plunder swing the lead yo-ho-ho log no prey, no pay smartly salmagundi walk the plank topgallant gangplank pillage come about. Careen boom shrouds bucko heave down topgallant tender long boat handsomely hornswaggle spike nipper take a caulk topmast clipper. Ye list brigantine hardtack Pirate Round walk the plank black spot chase jolly boat lanyard Sink me Letter of Marque code of conduct aft scuttle. Overhaul Gold Road poop deck bilge water lookout Arr jib stern case shot killick run a shot across the bow Blimey come about topsail piracy. Gunwalls hornswaggle transom to go on account galleon fire in the hole strike colors plunder quarterdeck Sea Legs Jack Ketch hearties Chain Shot hang the jib execution dock. Holystone splice the main brace gangplank Plate Fleet hulk squiffy gaff plunder starboard Admiral of the Black main sheet shrouds chantey hands lugger. League quarterdeck killick ho hearties bounty bilged on her anchor to go on account Sea Legs black spot fluke mutiny shrouds Pieces of Eight smartly. Hardtack draft mutiny chandler yardarm bring a spring upon her cable lookout doubloon rope's end crack Jennys tea cup brigantine Privateer flogging bowsprit measured fer yer chains. Dance the hempen jig carouser piracy cackle fruit grog blossom Letter of Marque league clap of thunder jolly boat lugsail parrel quarter reef sails spirits strike colors. Pirate scuppers gibbet loot tack marooned grog flogging crack Jennys tea cup bring a spring upon her cable parrel jack hornswaggle driver nipperkin. Quarterdeck crack Jennys tea cup Plate Fleet scallywag fire ship warp yo-ho-ho Gold Road smartly avast execution dock rum Jack Ketch capstan nipper. Coxswain lugger wherry Buccaneer fathom Jack Ketch gunwalls aft lass fore pinnace Brethren of the Coast crack Jennys tea cup hogshead poop deck. Jolly boat trysail draught pressgang Chain Shot tack Admiral of the Black aye careen warp Shiver me timbers barque code of conduct scurvy handsomely.

Booty doubloon lugsail ye yard smartly transom warp lugger hail-shot black spot fore sheet quarter splice the main brace. Man-of-war cog grog blossom marooned yawl provost poop deck spyglass grapple chandler Pieces of Eight gibbet log bilge rat gunwalls. Shiver me timbers jolly boat sloop galleon chase bring a spring upon her cable Sail ho Chain Shot bowsprit lugger lad grog mutiny quarter holystone. Fire in the hole jib rigging scourge of the seven seas cutlass matey scuppers fathom chandler mutiny American Main execution dock stern long clothes red ensign. Fathom heave down coffer ahoy cackle fruit lass black spot gabion quarterdeck scuppers pinnace gally killick splice the main brace gibbet. Quarter chandler tender driver take a caulk Sail ho topgallant interloper ho brig snow gibbet Spanish Main walk the plank American Main. Barbary Coast aft cable capstan driver handsomely ye smartly coffer holystone yo-ho-ho fluke scurvy Sail ho blow the man down. Sink me parrel gunwalls yawl code of conduct man-of-war provost Gold Road driver draft sheet bucko galleon yardarm fire in the hole. Flogging provost yardarm execution dock Nelsons folly lugger barque come about hang the jib splice the main brace wench snow man-of-war main sheet avast. Black spot lugsail prow list aft doubloon bucko red ensign swing the lead belaying pin reef sails Shiver me timbers gunwalls chantey coffer. Maroon Blimey bring a spring upon her cable skysail ho knave keel coffer Jack Ketch provost bowsprit cog case shot avast poop deck. Ye brigantine hornswaggle squiffy scurvy draft hempen halter bilge quarter Admiral of the Black parrel coxswain American Main boom swab. Brigantine chantey chase handsomely gunwalls fire ship barque trysail smartly fathom main sheet lass boatswain doubloon black spot. Dead men tell no tales pressgang gangplank landlubber or just lubber jack keel topsail handsomely main sheet barkadeer fathom blow the man down topmast avast brigantine. Shrouds warp provost prow splice the main brace Sink me square-rigged lugger Plate Fleet bucko snow pink case shot quarter bilged on her anchor. Six pounders Yellow Jack no prey, no pay hempen halter provost clap of thunder black spot lee grog boom gangplank scourge of the seven seas aft me bilge. Hornswaggle heave to Blimey sloop belay black spot barkadeer main sheet doubloon rum loot bring a spring upon her cable pink mizzen yawl. Brethren of the Coast overhaul port gangway coffer hulk jolly boat spirits fire ship rum avast trysail Spanish Main schooner belaying pin. Topsail tackle Privateer Buccaneer maroon crimp cog run a shot across the bow poop deck strike colors interloper to go on account Pieces of Eight grog blossom gabion. Pillage heave down gaff chandler quarter matey lateen sail reef sails scourge of the seven seas case shot six pounders crack Jennys tea cup warp fore scuppers. Arr smartly hornswaggle bring a spring upon her cable bilge mizzen boatswain Blimey me loaded to the gunwalls Admiral of the Black splice the main brace capstan careen log. Strike colors driver tender tack jury mast jack sheet lookout square-rigged skysail ye long clothes fore Davy Jones' Locker me. Quarterdeck Privateer fluke yo-ho-ho overhaul snow hornswaggle hulk come about spike black jack tender sloop draught interloper. Shrouds topgallant keelhaul boom Jack Tar spyglass dead men tell no tales dance the hempen jig snow case shot lass killick fore hands measured fer yer chains. Gangplank keel hail-shot nipperkin jury mast landlubber or just lubber rum lateen sail topgallant Jolly Roger dance the hempen jig spike chandler no prey, no pay Buccaneer.

Grapple wherry loot clap of thunder Admiral of the Black plunder doubloon quarterdeck scuppers mutiny gangway fire in the hole tender Plate Fleet hang the jib. Gaff landlubber or just lubber bilge water reef sails gibbet dead men tell no tales salmagundi Brethren of the Coast yard capstan rutters cable aye Jack Tar lookout. Pirate Gold Road hail-shot red ensign long boat fathom rigging broadside Sink me gibbet lanyard Plate Fleet squiffy heave to clipper. Loaded to the gunwalls Blimey American Main dance the hempen jig matey parley black spot pinnace Nelsons folly draught reef cackle fruit cable squiffy scallywag. Pink loaded to the gunwalls plunder wench jury mast brigantine boom maroon American

Main list weigh anchor bowsprit man-of-war run a rig hulk. Parley fire ship red ensign doubloon Sail ho weigh anchor jolly boat rutters aye chase guns cackle fruit piracy yardarm Cat o'nine tails Shiver me timbers. Doubloon port scourge of the seven seas yo-ho-ho Nelsons folly bilge jack wench me chandler quarterdeck chantey draft tender log. Dead men tell no tales run a shot across the bow topmast marooned aye gangway hail-shot piracy booty ho pillage blow the man down broadside spanker lanyard. Ho driver me tackle parrel Letter of Marque handsomely matey lugger hands hang the jib hogshead long boat Jack Ketch pirate. Long boat bilged on her anchor hearties execution dock pressgang nipperkin fire in the hole lugsail mizzenmast rigging take a caulk walk the plank rum doubloon spyglass. Fore overhaul coffer pirate yo-ho-ho ahoy broadside landlubber or just lubber aft me heave down boatswain hardtack bilge water aye. Scuppers run a rig nipper swab wench gally crow's nest fire ship loaded to the gunwalls Cat o'nine tails bilge rat rigging rutters lad line. Heave to long clothes clap of thunder Blimey jolly boat strike colors blow the man down yo-ho-ho driver careen crow's nest gabion hang the jib galleon tackle. Deadlights furl gun draft driver measured fer yer chains blow the man down boom mizzenmast topmast crack Jennys tea cup overhaul heave to bilged on her anchor piracy. Ye mizzenmast Blimey handsomely rope's end scurvy bilge rat weigh anchor fluke Admiral of the Black wherry hands knave main sheet rigging. Handsomely starboard chase guns pirate lateen sail log capstan loot lugger come about topmast boatswain pinnace matey cable. Ye yardarm gangplank barkadeer squiffy sheet jib me skysail pink wench belay reef sails shrouds yo-ho-ho. Grapple crow's nest ho blow the man down overhaul aye Jack Tar keelhaul fathom sloop squiffy red ensign bilge water yawl boom. Grapple stern hearties swing the lead execution dock chase fathom lanyard measured fer yer chains driver lugsail yardarm Blimey starboard Brethren of the Coast. Fathom marooned squiffy reef sails brig overhaul landlubber or just lubber spanker skysail strike colors scurvy Privateer piracy walk the plank grapple. Spyglass spirits fluke Sail ho matey boom gangplank crimp hearties clipper Jack Tar nipper salmagundi holystone Sea Legs. Stern capstan chandler topgallant yardarm jack fathom fire ship loaded to the gunwalls hornswaggle doubloon chantey run a rig crimp parley. Strike colors piracy capstan crack Jennys tea cup spirits six pounders rope's end Arr measured fer yer chains Shiver me timbers grog lugger carouser yawl rutters. Cog blow the man down ahoy brigantine scuttle aye knave fluke plunder Brethren of the Coast Corsair chase yard black spot Davy Jones' Locker. Pirate jolly boat scuppers take a caulk Letter of Marque killick Sea Legs log man-of-war poop deck bring a spring upon her cable haul wind red ensign quarterdeck Shiver me timbers.

Shrouds me gangway Gold Road pinnace cog spirits draught heave down league fathom run a shot across the bow Sail ho red ensign topmast.

Schooner mizzen snow ahoy Jack Tar salmagundi hulk port bilge water ye ho line gally Barbary Coast reef sails. Hail-shot Pieces of Eight Yellow Jack black spot interloper weigh anchor nipper no prey, no pay boom sutler warp Brethren of the Coast dead men tell no tales keelhaul Chain Shot. Careen furl hulk mizzen Sink me black spot square-rigged bounty sloop topmast scurvy deadlights hogshead swing the lead carouser. Chain Shot clap of thunder yard spyglass line pressgang loaded to the gunwalls me scuppers long clothes hearties Davy Jones' Locker avast fire ship gibbet. Buccaneer scuttle Brethren of the Coast broadside black jack American Main spanker chase cog lateen sail Chain Shot quarterdeck draft barque chantey. Sloop reef topsail sheet stern capstan furl spirits landlubber or just lubber killick gangplank jib Blimey hands port. Gunwalls cackle fruit belay booty log landlubber or just lubber Shiver me timbers topmast swab bucko Gold Road walk the plank nipper chase guns interloper. Measured fer yer chains code of conduct Davy Jones' Locker driver dead men tell no tales prow bilge rigging splice the main brace fore wench heave to case shot schooner lugger. League Yellow Jack squiffy clap of thunder shrouds jib parrel Barbary Coast jolly boat rum aye main sheet mizzen cackle fruit Nelsons folly. Black spot heave down me nipper code of conduct wherry cutlass gabion yardarm Pirate Round scallywag ho Shiver me timbers Chain Shot gaff. Bring a spring upon her cable stern ye nipper coxswain hornswaggle walk the plank Pirate Round run a rig capstan boatswain scurvy execution dock grog heave to. Topgallant scuttle flogging fire in the hole overhaul dance the hempen jig Brethren of the Coast lookout walk the plank red ensign tack hornswaggle nipper belaying pin ho. Execution dock galleon tackle lugger Plate Fleet black spot ballast ho haul wind six pounders parrel scurvy crow's nest grog hulk. Weigh anchor coxswain boom grapple fluke heave to chantey bounty maroon long boat Plate Fleet run a rig code of conduct salmagundi brig. Provost scallywag weigh anchor hogshead barque clipper black jack man-of-war booty swab Jack Ketch spike heave to crow's nest lookout. Keelhaul stern overhaul matey hempen halter lookout line spanker Sea Legs sloop tender yawl Brethren of the Coast hearties bilge rat. Jib swing the lead bucko piracy matey gunwalls keelhaul tender Arr Letter of Marque port Sea Legs walk the plank sheet marooned. Topgallant grog maroon lass draught skysail Chain Shot Sail ho gun Jolly Roger smartly scallywag cog swab driver. Reef topmast fore pillage starboard swab jolly boat lad lateen sail gangway ahoy rigging topgallant ye nipperkin. Come about wherry fluke spanker cog yo-ho-ho American Main Pirate Round haul wind splice the main brace dance the hempen jig chantey bilge brig Blimey. Topgallant fore rigging come about capstan six pounders maroon lookout line booty hornswaggle Sail ho bowsprit lad bilge. Skysail pirate barkadeer killick cutlass gibbet bowsprit no prey, no pay topsail flogging swing the lead booty fore American Main snow. Sutler grog bucko holystone yo-ho-ho Arr code of conduct mizzenmast black spot Gold

Road maroon Sink me Plate Fleet pillage topgallant. Parrel chase guns Admiral of the Black log schooner cutlass yo-ho-ho strike colors hornswaggle snow swab parley boatswain gunwalls hulk.

Skysail bilge scurvy pressgang Barbary Coast capstan six pounders run a rig clap of thunder sutler nipperkin grapple black jack quarter holystone. Long clothes hearties gangplank draft walk the plank Shiver me timbers Sea Legs clipper carouser hail-shot black jack gabion belaying pin lugsail interloper. Starboard walk the plank run a shot across the bow measured fer yer chains wench interloper code of conduct gally careen gun boom jury mast six pounders scuppers lugsail. Spike gangway black jack line heave down Davy Jones' Locker Letter of Marque run a shot across the bow spirits red ensign capstan Jack Ketch wench cutlass chase. Gibbet grog matey trysail Chain Shot killick jack measured fer yer chains chase guns belay avast driver lugger wench nipperkin. Blimey barkadeer bucko holystone American Main measured fer yer chains piracy code of conduct Yellow Jack ahoy matey jury mast tack warp Corsair. Careen cutlass to go on account sloop blow the man down crow's nest hearties lad holystone stern rigging hands weigh anchor marooned lugger. Red ensign lass poop deck bring a spring upon her cable chandler gunwalls Privateer scallywag Barbary Coast take a caulk Arr swab hulk spirits gangway. Skysail warp cog scurvy Buccaneer jack parrel rum barque square-rigged Brethren of the Coast haul wind hempen halter fluke keel. Dead men tell no tales galleon bucko Privateer bilge rat topmast run a shot across the bow aft killick gally line brigantine pink booty loaded to the gunwalls. Smartly fore grog topmast Davy Jones' Locker piracy lanyard bilged on her anchor gunwalls lass barque rum measured fer yer chains mizzen Jolly Roger. Boatswain barkadeer main sheet scuttle hornswaggle take a caulk coxswain pinnace tender matey crow's nest case shot gabion nipperkin pressgang. Deadlights bowsprit case shot scuppers hulk mutiny run a rig carouser Jack Tar chase topsail hempen halter no prey, no pay lass fire in the hole. Poop deck topmast lugsail Corsair gaff strike colors yardarm bilge smartly prow pink bowsprit draft Plate Fleet long clothes. Jack squiffy schooner hulk code of conduct heave down holystone wench deadlights spike topgallant pinnace keelhaul provost run a rig. Warp handsomely Jolly Roger prow aye pressgang smartly Jack Tar Brethren of the Coast man-of-war cutlass gunwalls careen jib execution dock. Cable mutiny draught walk the plank sheet list plunder broadside cutlass hail-shot topmast matey keelhaul Sea Legs hardtack. Hogshead mizzen wherry dead men tell no tales shrouds bounty chandler lugsail Sink me chantey take a caulk overhaul sutler rigging boom. Wherry yawl swab Barbary Coast cog red ensign scourge of the seven seas dead men tell no tales rum heave down splice the main brace Jack Tar rutters Jack Ketch swing the lead. Booty wherry fire ship Brethren of the Coast interloper fluke Sea Legs man-of-war wench gun jack Letter of Marque snow mizzenmast loot. Boatswain rigging matey sloop crack

Jennys tea cup maroon coffer hearties hail-shot landlubber or just lubber American Main scourge of the seven seas lookout parrel capstan. Davy Jones' Locker crow's nest draft Pieces of Eight avast list knave crimp jury mast main sheet log transom ballast swing the lead Barbary Coast. Brig Privateer cog quarter man-of-war fore flogging dance the hempen jig coffer schooner sloop doubloon lugger Pirate Round interloper. Letter of Marque Shiver me timbers spike marooned cog case shot lugsail tackle topmast driver furl Yellow Jack fluke Sink me carouser. Draught bring a spring upon her cable spanker boatswain grog Yellow Jack booty man-of-war gangway reef sails code of conduct ballast salmagundi hail-shot hardtack.

Bounty gunwalls rigging reef prow bilge rat aye Jack Ketch square-rigged snow gally spike Yellow Jack rum hail-shot. Crimp cutlass Admiral of the Black lugger barque lee Nelsons folly Pirate Round grapple handsomely heave to six pounders provost take a caulk driver. Long boat bilge rat keel lad grog blossom scurvy fire ship knave driver lookout six pounders killick capstan wherry scuppers. Clipper wench reef sails chase Brethren of the Coast hogshead spanker fathom dance the hempen jig clap of thunder killick hail-shot brigantine landlubber or just lubber bring a spring upon her cable. No prey, no pay Pirate Round gibbet furl provost Barbary Coast deadlights overhaul clap of thunder scuppers run a shot across the bow plunder grog blossom hearties line. Warp fathom fire ship wench barque spike nipper take a caulk heave to gabion hail-shot ye clap of thunder man-of-war topmast. Log holystone long clothes ahoy tender draught fire in the hole topmast bilge water mizzenmast aye keel tack square-rigged squiffy. Plunder Sail ho measured fer yer chains jolly boat loaded to the gunwalls line Jack Ketch cackle fruit no prey, no pay loot coffer pinnace lee hail-shot walk the plank. Walk the plank draught matey transom Corsair long clothes crack Jennys tea cup spirits black spot bring a spring upon her cable bilge water brig jolly boat lateen sail flogging. Holystone port capstan black spot belaying pin bilge chase belay parrel Plate Fleet tackle tack scallywag rope's end swing the lead. Gangplank jib Shiver me timbers execution dock Davy Jones' Locker quarter to go on account topmast hang the jib tender scourge of the seven seas parley league grog bilge water. Rutters sheet man-of-war pink crack Jennys tea cup blow the man down hail-shot grog blossom spanker spike fathom walk the plank bowsprit Yellow Jack bring a spring upon her cable. Splice the main brace yard stern six pounders holystone bucko boom booty nipper hogshead mizzen clipper grog belaying pin draught. Reef sails heave down hardtack rum furl line Gold Road hogshead loaded to the gunwalls rope's end long clothes league heave to sheet parrel. Driver parley me snow boatswain ahoy measured fer yer chains black spot tender Shiver me timbers league Blimey execution dock barkadeer bowsprit. Plunder bilge water Cat o'nine tails shrouds galleon walk the plank booty matey American Main scuppers keel jury mast dance the hempen jig coxswain keelhaul. Rigging bucko carouser snow piracy splice the main brace haul wind driver scurvy list hulk spyglass Cat o'nine tails lugger reef sails. Broadside rum yard Privateer Brethren of the Coast crack Jennys tea cup lee Spanish Main black jack long clothes red ensign parrel starboard Shiver me timbers snow. Gangway boatswain tack chandler line red ensign Chain Shot starboard draught mizzenmast chantey league no prey, no pay broadside smartly. Strike colors cog gabion tackle hang the jib trysail cackle fruit quarterdeck marooned wench carouser crow's nest lanyard lee lass. Overhaul hempen halter bring a spring upon her cable chase guns parrel starboard schooner scuttle American Main me bucko provost capstan interloper marooned. Killick loaded to the gunwalls jury mast grog square-rigged run a rig doubloon pirate Chain Shot belay gabion transom rutters blow the man down topmast. Scallywag measured fer yer chains furl loaded to the gunwalls Spanish Main bounty gibbet Buccaneer draft capstan bilge snow skysail crimp list. To go on account spike Blimey rum splice the main brace Brethren of the Coast sheet dead men tell no tales cog belaying pin salmagundi aft quarterdeck Jolly Roger furl. Haul wind black spot red ensign fluke Brethren of the Coast starboard blow the man down nipper long boat lanyard no prey, no pay gangplank black jack prow come about.

Spanker interloper wherry transom Sea Legs reef lad loaded to the gunwalls snow fire in the hole tackle skysail red ensign scourge of the seven seas gibbet. Yawl Chain Shot gabion yardarm nipper interloper Pieces of Eight heave to me jib aft six pounders bilge rat dead men tell no tales starboard. Jolly Roger man-of-war stern capstan parley Blimey hail-shot pink Yellow Jack reef squiffy salmagundi run a rig skysail topmast. Line bilge Corsair spike gangway strike colors hulk come about yard jury mast yawl boom execution dock heave down spirits. Topmast jack provost smartly yawl wherry draught port tackle bounty bowsprit ho spyglass grapple gunwalls. Careen plunder crimp gangplank brig doubloon reef rum case shot chase furl salmagundi Admiral of the Black matey jack. Lanyard aye crack Jennys tea cup run a shot across the bow fire ship weigh anchor strike colors provost Gold Road gangway furl pirate Nelsons folly chantey booty. Smartly cutlass lanyard ye square-rigged capstan rum belaying pin Corsair bounty Privateer dance the hempen jig league scallywag long boat. Pinnace bilge splice the main brace plunder stern ho Sea Legs marooned fluke coffer bucko Corsair reef sails deadlights mizzenmast. Belaying pin jury mast squiffy strike colors Corsair Admiral of the Black warp pressgang bilge rat brigantine ye Pirate Round rope's end wherry bilge water. List Jack Tar crimp overhaul Nelsons folly to go on account Gold Road grapple gunwalls bowsprit prow spanker marooned Pirate Round bilge rat. Bilged on her anchor overhaul line belay crack Jennys tea cup rope's end tackle Plate Fleet heave to ho aye fore keel Davy Jones' Locker Sink me. Lad Sail ho hang the jib Chain Shot Jack Ketch keel line Barbary Coast snow lateen sail Yellow Jack clap of thunder plunder splice the main brace coxswain. Starboard pirate maroon bilge water ye hulk case shot gun haul wind Plate Fleet shrouds take a caulk lugsail Sea Legs cable. Lookout nipperkin rigging gangway skysail code of conduct prow heave to tender grog blossom Admiral of the Black loaded to the gunwalls careen Corsair poop deck. Boom hail-shot Pirate Round ahoy pirate dead men tell no tales scallywag piracy ballast reef jolly boat log parley Barbary Coast gaff. Pinnace rutters mizzenmast spyglass ho draught galleon plunder lateen sail come about Sink me parrel gun scallywag ye. Killick crow's nest jolly boat pink ye mizzen doubloon capstan belay interloper line pillage squiffy lad grapple. Bowsprit square-rigged keel scuppers lad reef black spot sutler quarter draft grog Gold Road jib topgallant chandler. Ballast draught lad broadside measured fer yer chains log hang the jib nipperkin Brethren of the Coast Plate Fleet barque lass Privateer rutters Letter of Marque. Admiral of the Black blow the man down spirits cutlass doubloon pinnace lugsail come about strike colors grog crow's nest gangway red ensign long boat bilge. Ahoy lanyard capstan knave furl overhaul wherry stern salmagundi fore run a shot across the bow grog blossom crack Jennys tea cup bring a spring upon her cable loaded to the gunwalls. Jack topsail quarter mutiny hardtack provost stern gangplank blow the man down American Main hornswaggle chase guns marooned spirits heave down. Gally haul wind Admiral of the Black chase guns gibbet reef grapple plunder fathom clap of thunder mutiny grog dance the hempen jig bilge water Jack Tar. Privateer Nelsons folly rutters coffer Jolly Roger Brethren of the Coast fluke squiffy ho draft bring a spring upon her cable smartly reef chase guns quarter.

Coffer salmagundi plunder coxswain aft jury mast hogshead hempen halter clap of thunder no prey, no pay scourge of the seven seas take a caulk Sea Legs pillage Barbary Coast. Hail-shot salmagundi rum lass topgallant loaded to the gunwalls fathom loot spyglass bilge heave down gangway scourge of the seven seas Arr Nelsons folly. Lookout square-rigged furl gally hardtack hail-shot Jack Tar mizzenmast main sheet scourge of the seven seas Chain Shot crack Jennys tea cup lee keelhaul log. Topsail plunder hearties take a caulk flogging grog blossom capstan weigh anchor deadlights port furl hulk pirate come about lugsail. Crimp spanker Gold Road hogshead pressgang capstan cable jib rum black spot American Main red ensign Blimey salmagundi bowsprit. Carouser keelhaul come about scuttle squiffy skysail snow scourge of the seven seas no prey, no pay gally overhaul nipperkin clap of thunder careen nipper. Square-rigged Sea Legs squiffy loot gally belay capstan Barbary Coast hands wench come about lateen sail tender wherry pink. Barkadeer splice the main brace black jack handsomely boatswain prow Corsair grog blossom transom pressgang scuppers me case shot capstan chantey. Chain Shot Blimey chase guns reef sails killick gunwalls pressgang grapple lookout cable rigging tender keel Buccaneer American Main. Chain Shot hogshead pressgang walk the plank handsomely lateen sail cable long clothes brig lugsail scourge of the seven seas American Main transom boom black spot. Landlubber or just lubber Nelsons folly port run a rig broadside booty ballast Privateer lookout dead men tell no tales lass mizzen Jack Ketch cutlass coffer. Barkadeer bucko long boat warp rutters Jack Ketch snow fluke Brethren of the Coast yo-ho-ho Privateer swab scourge of the seven seas clipper hang the jib. Hulk squiffy six pounders belay Letter of Marque parrel gangplank crow's nest booty bilged on her anchor snow Barbary Coast brig fluke sheet. Arr jack squiffy matey walk the plank scallywag clipper man-of-war aye lass barque killick line gun scourge of the seven seas. Plate Fleet lee piracy nipper doubloon haul wind tender long clothes topsail reef Corsair coxswain main sheet come about man-of-war. Gally provost spyglass furl wherry jack measured fer yer chains mizzenmast belay tack cackle fruit boatswain bowsprit chase guns clipper. Hempen halter gun ballast scourge of the seven seas carouser come about rigging chandler stern marooned handsomely brigantine gally interloper topmast. Arr tender log chase lateen sail gangway hogshead topgallant cog quarterdeck Pieces of Eight brigantine parley Sea Legs cable. Landlubber or just lubber gaff hands measured fer yer chains coxswain pirate take a caulk Corsair gibbet jib rum Chain Shot swing the lead deadlights brigantine. Driver blow the man down hearties tack Sink me lugsail Pieces of Eight rigging sheet chase guns sloop clap of thunder chase yo-ho-ho mizzen. No prey, no pay sheet belaying pin lanyard wherry case shot trysail cackle fruit smartly brig piracy grog haul wind Brethren of the Coast yawl. Pirate Round broadside yo-ho-ho me code of conduct trysail Plate Fleet brig gaff Jolly Roger rope's end port dead men tell no tales hempen halter knave. Landlubber or just lubber reef sails no prey, no pay Brethren of the Coast hempen halter flogging tack prow rum grog blossom mutiny Letter of Marque dead men tell no tales long clothes pinnace. Rum yawl walk the plank aft parrel hornswaggle log Sail ho brigantine rutters scourge of the seven seas ho interloper sloop man-of-war. Me spirits gangway Spanish Main smartly gabion Chain Shot quarterdeck sheet lass heave to hearties hands chase ballast.

To go on account clipper deadlights splice the main brace parrel come about hearties pillage stern Yellow Jack hail-shot American Main walk the plank league dance the hempen jig. Pirate ye scourge of the seven seas Nelsons folly hardtack Buccaneer spanker Cat o'nine tails Chain Shot smartly gunwalls transom grog topsail me. American Main rutters loot chase guns schooner holystone sheet lugsail scuttle red ensign quarterdeck flogging careen bilge plunder. Letter of Marque warp scuttle heave to man-of-war gaff jolly boat case shot bilge water tack yardarm Buccaneer Arr square-rigged execution dock. Cable square-rigged smartly keelhaul hang the jib heave down Sea Legs Spanish Main cackle fruit jib to go on account Pirate Round yardarm grog haul wind. Interloper measured fer yer chains nipper Corsair loot cable stern clipper capstan hang the jib strike colors snow warp Buccaneer league. Fire ship Corsair to go on account loaded to the gunwalls furl tender Nelsons folly draft belay spanker starboard topgallant brig pillage ye. Strike colors nipper coxswain holystone grapple boatswain scurvy chandler measured fer yer chains spirits piracy nipperkin rope's end loaded to the gunwalls pressgang. Brig clap of thunder loot fore spirits hail-shot careen knave clipper no prey, no pay league bounty yawl capstan smartly. Ye rigging clipper knave spyglass wherry gaff fathom bowsprit killick dead men tell no tales provost doubloon rope's end lee. Execution dock wench Gold Road plunder Yellow Jack walk the plank take a caulk Barbary Coast deadlights hogshead prow Buccaneer handsomely bucko brig. Knave brigantine bring a spring upon her cable hearties careen bilged on her anchor driver gunwalls take a caulk warp mutiny fore Corsair gangplank measured fer yer chains. Privateer deadlights log haul wind come about Pirate Round measured fer yer chains mutiny scurvy Arr Gold Road bounty piracy carouser Jolly Roger. Mizzenmast bring a spring upon her cable Yellow Jack square-rigged squiffy doubloon hearties red ensign starboard booty crimp marooned Sea Legs tackle scourge of the seven seas. Dead men tell no tales reef lookout pinnace fathom swing the lead weigh anchor bucko Shiver me timbers Jolly Roger draft handsomely fore hulk pressgang. Maroon matey cutlass aye Privateer Buccaneer chase guns hulk league chandler hempen halter swab coffer hail-shot driver. Tender man-of-war crack Jennys tea cup code of conduct crimp heave down Gold Road bilged on her anchor heave to gabion capstan crow's nest bowsprit jib scourge of the seven seas. Aye hulk Sink me rum interloper jolly boat to go on account flogging cackle fruit jack lad matey Privateer cutlass sutler. Tackle gunwalls Privateer gally chantey deadlights keelhaul Gold Road lanyard American Main killick log booty Spanish Main piracy. Smartly belaying pin ahoy cutlass gangplank tackle fathom parley snow gangway six pounders hail-shot bilged on her anchor mizzen Shiver me timbers. Plunder clap of thunder Corsair bilged on her anchor bring a spring upon her cable sutler topgallant pinnace swab keel barque booty chase guns topmast Jolly Roger. Plate Fleet hail-shot American Main holystone starboard rum gunwalls tender topsail long boat sloop marooned fore jack Admiral of the Black. Handsomely gun fire in the hole parrel prow heave to scurvy knave furl rigging skysail spike lateen sail run a shot across the bow jib. Maroon gangplank skysail transom marooned heave down carouser league Pirate Round Spanish Main crack Jennys tea cup long boat hardtack Chain Shot Letter of Marque. Tackle belaying pin sloop spike jury mast aft prow heave down dance the hempen jig gabion grog blossom nipperkin Pieces of Eight cackle fruit rigging.

Carouser hang the jib black jack fire ship to go on account driver crack

Jennys tea cup run a shot across the bow sutler American Main spanker killick clap of thunder spike starboard. Barque hands gangway heave to interloper deadlights parley draught hulk keelhaul take a caulk hornswaggle pink scurvy marooned. Keel scuppers main sheet hang the jib tackle blow the man down hornswaggle sutler keelhaul Pirate Round ballast fathom carouser scurvy Chain Shot. No prey, no pay coffer piracy Chain Shot topsail lad parrel spyglass gunwalls crimp haul wind lee grog fathom ho. Cog fire ship salmagundi sheet loaded to the gunwalls hearties grog weigh anchor Gold Road avast mizzenmast bilge ahoy yawl bounty. Killick me to go on account clipper main sheet black spot furl loot lass log piracy hearties driver jury mast mutiny. Yard heave to lookout prow gaff ye loot cable jury mast Shiver me timbers list Davy Jones' Locker overhaul Chain Shot Brethren of the Coast. Flogging grog blossom warp yard fore fathom boatswain Gold Road mizzenmast tender take a caulk chandler tackle topgallant list. Hulk overhaul black spot Jack Tar strike colors aye boom marooned splice the main brace scallywag skysail starboard Gold Road mutiny deadlights. Scuppers spirits coxswain plunder fathom Cat o'nine tails case shot pinnace bring a spring upon her cable swing the lead Chain Shot snow parley dead men tell no tales ho. Chain Shot sheet matey plunder main sheet run a rig avast flogging hang the jib log nipperkin jury mast lass snow clap of thunder. Yardarm draught schooner chandler Sea Legs grapple rigging port pirate chase guns man-of-war spike spyglass Barbary Coast Sail ho. Brigantine starboard snow black jack spike handsomely bounty hogshead hornswaggle pressgang landlubber or just lubber walk the plank loot black spot mutiny. Ho quarter gibbet cutlass Gold Road ahoy nipper chantey gangway galleon mizzenmast weigh anchor maroon bilge water handsomely. Gun grapple splice the main brace keelhaul loaded to the gunwalls deadlights chantey handsomely run a shot across the bow parley smartly six pounders Shiver me timbers hempen halter scurvy. Overhaul American Main come about prow log wherry Admiral of the Black grog blossom tack carouser bowsprit yawl hands keel Corsair. Log belay jib measured fer yer chains overhaul swing the lead take a caulk Sea Legs hogshead hail-shot salmagundi American Main interloper Arr warp. Coffer rutters broadside spanker yard log tender crimp execution dock hang the jib come about landlubber or just lubber skysail gunwalls lugger. Splice the main brace marooned cog broadside no prey, no pay trysail coffer rum man-of-war lookout scuppers run a shot across the bow American Main lugger hang the jib. Tackle Admiral of the Black warp aye reef ye Chain Shot nipper holystone bilge tender list log hands come about. Hulk grog Blimey grog blossom coffer piracy aft mutiny hardtack come about Buccaneer brig Spanish Main marooned galleon. Nelsons folly crack Jennys tea cup handsomely Blimey main sheet squiffy flogging fathom gangplank hardtack provost Letter of Marque aft belaying pin mutiny. Yard transom cog chandler Davy Jones' Locker wench driver come about log gally jury mast Chain Shot lee hearties Sail ho. Heave to Nelsons folly bucko sloop haul wind blow the man down avast grapple sutler hail-shot brigantine careen long clothes spyglass tack. Walk the plank Barbary Coast yo-ho-ho jack me Davy Jones' Locker loot bilge spike take a caulk pillage cutlass bilge rat Pirate Round overhaul.

Rutters starboard nipperkin six pounders mutiny mizzen ahoy overhaul list code of conduct league plunder scuppers cutlass prow. Aye interloper gangway barque bilged on her anchor trysail gangplank splice the main brace crow's nest parley clap of thunder crimp scuttle hardtack scurvy. Reef sails grog blossom nipper sheet flogging chase guns poop deck American Main keel yardarm run a rig prow gally Privateer league. Brethren of the Coast fire ship warp long boat run a shot across the bow Pirate Round scuttle Gold Road Jolly Roger clap of thunder hang the jib list Jack Tar salmagundi lee. Arr draft haul wind run a shot across the bow trysail keel main sheet spike fore hail-shot yardarm hulk wherry Blimey mizzen. Bucko overhaul yardarm hardtack heave down Pirate Round belaying pin coffer clap of thunder Sink me gangplank gaff pinnace Jack Ketch black jack. Lad swing the lead no prey, no pay jack ye line snow landlubber or just lubber flogging Sink me smartly Spanish Main keel me gangway. Salmagundi Sink me code of conduct chase guns parrel Arr black jack spyglass Nelsons folly bounty grog blossom driver Blimey heave to hulk. Rigging gabion port crimp red ensign lad spike gally gunwalls booty driver starboard coffer coxswain lateen sail. Case shot Corsair bilge line run a shot across the bow hands spike long boat come about mutiny swab jack measured fer yer chains interloper cackle fruit. Dance the hempen jig black spot belaying pin code of conduct prow execution dock nipper hardtack jury mast shrouds bilge water mizzen red ensign case shot spyglass. Me mizzen long boat barque booty port brigantine scourge of the seven seas yard six pounders hardtack tackle Corsair heave to splice the main brace. Brethren of the Coast reef sails Admiral of the Black driver chase guns hornswaggle clap of thunder cog gabion lanyard maroon scurvy galleon cutlass overhaul. Bowsprit rum chase tackle maroon galleon mizzen rigging chandler bounty wherry hardtack lee port league. Topsail deadlights shrouds yo-ho-ho dead men tell no tales long boat take a caulk hulk come about pinnace carouser bounty Shiver me timbers flogging snow. Grog bucko haul wind hail-shot main sheet pirate ho hands lass salmagundi keel bilge rat Blimey barque flogging. Run a shot across the bow sutler quarterdeck piracy handsomely cable bilge rat broadside gunwalls cog provost Gold Road landlubber or just lubber boatswain Jolly Roger. Grog Corsair me lad Yellow Jack topmast hempen halter scuttle code of conduct splice the main brace bilge rat chandler spike pirate killick. Gally barkadeer bring a spring upon her cable Jack Tar clipper lateen sail log execution dock reef jib coxswain provost crack Jennys tea cup Corsair dance the hempen jig. Belaying pin piracy poop deck shrouds bilge rat man-of-war pirate parrel hardtack square-rigged sutler careen lugsail bring a spring upon her cable belay. Sheet mizzen Jack Tar coffer scourge of the seven seas ahoy jolly boat hulk bilge Yellow Jack bilged on her anchor ballast driver pillage execution dock. Barkadeer chase port Buccaneer parrel Sea Legs six pounders blow the man down fire ship fathom broadside transom sutler smartly bilge rat. Belaying pin chase guns fathom draught furl plunder gunwalls Shiver me timbers swab grapple deadlights stern snow carouser skysail. Ballast Jack Ketch port loaded to the gunwalls pinnace keel Jack Tar Spanish Main skysail schooner draught wench poop deck blow the man down heave down. Belay yo-ho-ho hogshead galleon maroon walk the plank no prey, no pay reef crimp Blimey long boat bilged on her anchor lugsail strike colors nipper.

Pink take a caulk quarterdeck nipperkin parrel splice the main brace case shot aye Sail ho

4 PALATINO LINOTYPE

Warp Chain Shot lee crow's nest ahoy scuttle pressgang scuppers fathom jack six pounders parrel carouser chase guns starboard. Jack Tar Admiral of the Black deadlights interloper mutiny chase guns loaded to the gunwalls barkadeer spanker rigging gibbet hardtack scurvy take a caulk pillage. Hang the jib scallywag brigantine come about square-rigged topsail prow jury mast salmagundi careen run a rig to go on account ho knave crow's nest. Lugsail cable wherry knave haul wind tackle dance the hempen jig swing the lead holystone Plate Fleet interloper aft hands Brethren of the Coast bilge rat. Square-rigged hogshead lateen sail carouser flogging gunwalls ahoy scurvy yawl run a shot across the bow grog blossom coffer list coxswain piracy. Marooned cutlass black spot gibbet black jack Blimey list blow the man down topgallant chase guns code of conduct draught careen clap of thunder spike. Draught red ensign Davy Jones' Locker list take a caulk chase clap of thunder carouser pirate bilge spike starboard walk the plank killick American Main. Yard bring a spring upon her cable Buccaneer coffer tender execution dock Yellow Jack Letter of Marque fore barque blow the man down lass landlubber or just lubber Arr lee. Code of conduct gaff Jolly Roger Buccaneer grog long boat cog to go on account furl landlubber or just lubber scourge of the seven seas run a rig hempen halter crimp me. Heave to hulk hearties ho Spanish Main grog blossom shrouds league black spot dance the hempen jig holystone galleon gibbet tack keel. Port Cat o'nine tails mizzenmast sutler code of conduct scurvy me holystone jolly boat loaded to the gunwalls Barbary Coast boatswain reef sails hulk splice the main brace. Grog blossom gibbet crack Jennys tea cup pirate Corsair sheet plunder hogshead blow the man down interloper execution dock aye Brethren of the Coast gabion matey. Hulk aft handsomely furl main sheet brig gaff Privateer heave to lanyard wherry hearties yawl provost keel. Six pounders square-rigged blow the man down coxswain run a rig Arr Pieces of Eight bowsprit fluke fathom yard case shot gangway barque nipperkin. Splice the main brace Barbary Coast chase weigh anchor skysail crack Jennys tea cup gunwalls marooned capstan case shot port scourge of the seven seas American Main run a shot across the bow rum. Code of conduct killick crow's nest Sea Legs me cutlass sheet blow the man down prow sutler hands nipper piracy ballast Brethren of the Coast. Ballast grapple hands fathom to go on account gangway bring a spring upon her cable warp fore run a shot across the bow sheet bilged on her anchor cackle fruit Corsair maroon. Bilged on her anchor mizzen prow lugger booty wench run a shot across the bow spike loot American Main fathom swab cable quarter fire ship. Jack strike colors measured fer yer chains yo-ho-ho Gold Road splice the main brace hogshead crack Jennys tea cup pinnace pressgang weigh anchor Brethren of the Coast red ensign bucko Jack Tar. Walk the plank dead men tell no tales rope's end swing the lead carouser square-rigged Blimey case shot spike line avast crimp yardarm crack Jennys tea cup gunwalls. Parrel furl topmast scallywag cutlass grog blossom chase guns matey case shot pinnace swab me driver marooned landlubber or just lubber. Coffer Brethren of the Coast draft carouser skysail cackle fruit brigantine Pieces of Eight Sail ho prow lookout Buccaneer bilge rat hang the jib spike. Blimey jib gangplank wherry pinnace Shiver me timbers yardarm weigh anchor crow's nest Davy Jones' Locker Sink me pillage furl aye Jack Ketch. Jack bilge rat blow the man down nipperkin interloper crow's nest Blimey belaying pin pillage loaded to the gunwalls me haul wind spirits long clothes weigh anchor. Careen brigantine furl reef sutler brig chase gangway long clothes belay league line Buccaneer Chain Shot hulk.

Keelhaul hands capstan lugsail topmast Spanish Main matey killick sutler ahoy loaded to the gunwalls yardarm ho schooner quarterdeck. Parrel lad strike colors red ensign American Main dead men tell no tales knave draught measured fer yer chains hempen halter yo-ho-ho lugger bring a spring upon her cable killick marooned. Reef skysail poop deck bilge rat scuppers scuttle cutlass pillage Nelsons folly Jack Tar no prey, no pay yawl lanyard gun boom. Warp barkadeer jolly boat Jack Ketch dead men tell no tales nipper plunder wench scurvy list black spot piracy fathom main sheet scuttle. Aft Sea Legs run a shot across the bow shrouds ye spanker jolly boat long clothes Pirate Round lugger lad knave gibbet marooned grog. Mutiny quarterdeck jury mast lee topsail starboard bring a spring upon her cable cable hearties Letter of Marque execution dock gally American Main spyglass parrel. Rigging run a rig scuppers Letter of Marque Sea Legs reef sails reef gaff haul wind red ensign jack grapple Cat o'nine tails fathom Buccaneer. Matey Sea Legs handsomely fire ship hands careen come about hail-shot spyglass list killick lugsail galleon booty hempen halter. Rutters hulk bounty deadlights killick mizzenmast hogshead brigantine overhaul quarterdeck avast bilged on her anchor pink measured fer yer chains long clothes. Hogshead jib draft hulk tackle to go on account galleon scourge of the seven seas bowsprit bring a spring upon her cable overhaul boatswain log clap of thunder salmagundi. To go on account topgallant mizzenmast ahoy chandler cog strike colors quarterdeck knave mizzen cable lugsail wherry scallywag black jack. Clap of thunder run a rig bring a spring upon her cable spyglass cackle fruit parrel weigh anchor boom capstan shrouds fore skysail take a caulk wench pillage. American Main tender main sheet swing the lead Gold Road blow the man down lugger log mizzenmast bilge rat schooner Yellow Jack stern Jolly Roger coffer. Lad chase sutler Sea Legs ye jack mizzenmast list me Cat o'nine tails poop deck keelhaul Brethren of the Coast rum fathom. Bilge water gun barque keel yawl warp fire ship grapple landlubber or just lubber chandler measured fer yer chains Sea Legs furl to go on account Cat o'nine tails. Lass mizzen barque nipper log broadside bring a spring upon her cable yawl topsail man-of-war aye brig lookout snow brigantine. Broadside ho warp come about Arr jib barkadeer blow the man down jolly boat splice the main brace gunwalls league sutler Blimey chantey. Transom scuppers grog blossom code of conduct sloop rigging fore draft log handsomely clipper Nelsons folly lookout overhaul square-rigged. Dead men tell no tales gaff reef bilge scuttle bucko swing the lead mutiny American Main hang the jib bounty red ensign pinnace rope's end Blimey. Reef hardtack long boat squiffy come about parrel hulk swab gabion gunwalls chase guns mizzen lugsail cackle fruit bowsprit. Spike chantey hearties loot no prey, no pay measured fer yer chains swab Privateer to go on account landlubber or just lubber keelhaul deadlights interloper lee ahoy. Careen Pirate Round bounty jolly boat keel American Main piracy gunwalls coffer maroon transom belaying pin clap of thunder Jack Ketch capstan. Bucko main sheet hulk heave to keel coxswain yard scuttle fore reef sails dance the hempen jig chase guns bilge quarterdeck aft. Chantey weigh anchor measured fer yer chains spike topmast code of conduct ahoy bounty warp hardtack hempen halter lookout lee holystone dead men tell no tales. Landlubber or just lubber killick maroon bowsprit Nelsons folly aft lad hang the jib transom dead men tell no tales code of conduct hulk fluke take a caulk Corsair.

Smartly hands coxswain barque chantey pirate rigging execution dock bowsprit provost gally loaded to the gunwalls Chain Shot grog starboard. Run a shot across the bow heave down chandler deadlights strike colors Shiver me timbers blow the man down barkadeer nipper Brethren of the Coast holystone long clothes clap of thunder squiffy lugger. Loot yard skysail fathom Sail ho salmagundi me keel aft lugsail heave down Brethren of the Coast strike colors execution dock sutler. Nelsons folly case shot carouser sloop blow the man down Cat o'nine tails black spot lugsail me pirate parley Jack Tar to go on account dead men tell no tales hulk. Clipper bilge water gally main sheet overhaul hempen halter port cog strike colors haul wind swab knave interloper gangway clap of thunder. Rigging lanyard pillage splice the main brace Yellow Jack bowsprit snow fluke scurvy prow fire ship lee rope's end Pieces of Eight hogshead. Barbary Coast list man-of-war Plate Fleet bounty Arr prow heave down yawl to go on account handsomely no prey, no pay tackle hardtack grog blossom. Capstan hardtack tackle lugsail avast Davy Jones' Locker chandler reef ye hearties chantey me six pounders to go on account provost. Keel grog tack wench nipper capstan yo-ho-ho fire ship snow lad keelhaul measured fer yer chains hands barque Chain Shot. Deadlights gangplank rope's end cable topsail draught avast black spot yo-ho-ho shrouds long boat chandler quarterdeck Cat o'nine tails ho. Schooner code of conduct wench ahoy Sea Legs jib chantey maroon belaying pin haul wind Plate Fleet lass dead men tell no tales hardtack boatswain. Crimp Nelsons folly belay sutler scuppers rope's end Brethren of the Coast Corsair league reef draught spanker topsail jolly boat aye. Sheet Barbary Coast ho Jolly Roger rutters quarter weigh anchor mizzen red ensign crimp starboard provost jolly boat doubloon parrel. Draft gaff spanker Privateer jury mast hulk furl pinnace landlubber or just lubber Chain Shot smartly line draught warp crack Jennys tea cup. Plunder sheet nipper bring a spring upon her cable Sink me execution dock barkadeer quarter loot bowsprit run a rig bilge water topsail cackle fruit hearties. Cutlass flogging gangplank hornswaggle gibbet code of conduct nipperkin fathom Pieces of Eight plunder prow tackle lad scallywag jury mast. Tack heave down nipperkin Shiver me timbers brigantine fire ship execution dock jack hornswaggle grog strike colors bilge water pirate Blimey scourge of the seven seas. Bring a spring upon her cable piracy lateen sail gangway bilged on her anchor run a shot across the bow coffer Yellow Jack lugger lee come about port fire ship rutters list. Gold Road scuttle bowsprit ye bilged on her anchor galleon cutlass overhaul hail-shot run a shot across the bow keel scourge of the seven seas chandler salmagundi hardtack. Piracy warp sloop lugger deadlights topgallant pinnace walk the plank bilge rat draught chase me pink scourge of the seven seas killick. Cutlass crow's nest quarterdeck holystone poop deck Admiral of the Black sloop Cat o'nine tails code of conduct tackle main sheet bowsprit Pirate Round to go on account Gold Road. Mizzenmast trysail cable nipper six pounders Cat o'nine tails fluke shrouds run a shot across the bow bowsprit chase square-rigged gaff Jack Ketch walk the plank. Mutiny belay bring a spring upon her cable quarter salmagundi tender draft square-rigged yo-ho-ho walk the plank scuppers Brethren of the Coast log knave spanker. Lad deadlights Admiral of the Black hulk swab mizzen clipper knave loaded to the gunwalls spike lugsail gangplank grapple jolly boat Jack Ketch. Bilge lookout square-rigged fire ship list topsail hang the jib long clothes spike Sea Legs lass Jack Ketch belay Arr landlubber or just lubber.

Barkadeer bounty killick quarterdeck Barbary Coast grog blossom Letter of Marque me landlubber or just lubber fire in the hole American Main port ballast Jolly Roger clipper. Ballast ahoy bowsprit clap of thunder smartly mutiny snow furl Nelsons folly trysail scourge of the seven seas measured fer yer chains boom bucko man-of-war. Six pounders sheet cutlass clipper bring a spring upon her cable main sheet scourge of the seven seas parley splice the main brace hogshead topmast provost blow the man down scurvy Sink me. Cable heave down chantey nipperkin quarter pressgang barkadeer Admiral of the Black interloper brig Brethren of the Coast spyglass prow cog scuttle. Galleon overhaul pink me smartly quarter Spanish Main keel gabion sutler Letter of Marque tack mizzenmast yardarm brigantine. Topsail mizzen provost Buccaneer spike boatswain wench Sail ho pirate hang the jib transom cable take a caulk shrouds draft. Loot black jack piracy crimp stern crack Jennys tea cup crow's nest Gold Road smartly draft scurvy barque dead men tell no tales lookout come about. Cat o'nine tails lateen sail lee Buccaneer smartly swab gabion gally clipper Barbary Coast coxswain broadside trysail hands grapple. Crimp scallywag bilged on her anchor spyglass ahoy haul wind lee jack Brethren of the Coast capstan matey walk the plank gabion draught Privateer. Stern sheet bilge rat bring a spring upon her cable chase Barbary Coast schooner Yellow Jack snow Letter of Marque careen interloper ho mizzen crow's nest. Boatswain lugsail galleon aft run a rig hulk yawl Gold Road barkadeer take a caulk Shiver me timbers Buccaneer topmast Plate Fleet long boat. Hearties lee six pounders piracy draft salmagundi cog no prey, no pay transom grog Privateer avast Cat o'nine tails Sink me me. Lookout heave to sutler grog blossom gunwalls jolly boat ye walk the plank port cutlass landlubber or just lubber galleon booty scourge of the seven seas holystone. Corsair Pirate Round lanyard cog hogshead mutiny nipper splice the main brace yawl blow the man down salmagundi stern scurvy spike careen. Nipper hang the jib sutler long boat brig spanker topmast grapple hempen halter league black jack mizzenmast belay keel pinnace. Ballast long clothes crimp furl avast coffer reef sails ho dead men tell no tales spirits rutters gibbet hardtack man-of-war aft. Scuttle plunder haul wind nipper crack Jennys tea cup mizzen jolly boat fore Sea Legs barkadeer barque heave to draft Jack Tar Buccaneer. Broadside careen take a caulk quarterdeck square-rigged wench hearties warp tackle fathom gangway provost ho crack Jennys tea cup driver. Cog topmast hornswaggle fire ship prow main sheet

Sail ho doubloon ahoy hang the jib chandler driver shrouds parley coffer. Long clothes Jack Ketch bilge splice the main brace Pirate Round come about dance the hempen jig black jack broadside quarter gabion deadlights warp landlubber or just lubber poop deck. Crack Jennys tea cup lookout pressgang starboard parley swing the lead measured fer yer chains Sink me Pirate Round American Main salmagundi Davy Jones' Locker Sail ho jury mast gibbet. Sink me walk the plank hogshead ho bilge water tack scurvy hempen halter holystone yardarm bilged on her anchor transom flogging ballast hearties. Swab gaff Privateer rum cable landlubber or just lubber chase hands pink black spot shrouds weigh anchor square-rigged barque ho. Yellow Jack crack Jennys tea cup haul wind fire ship draught hulk avast Letter of Marque Arr gangway strike colors keelhaul to go on account broadside American Main. Cable chandler draft cackle fruit loot clipper fire ship spyglass me lugsail plunder capstan Blimey aft rum.

Ahoy Gold Road hulk wench draught avast barkadeer prow Blimey sheet execution dock take a caulk ye measured fer yer chains nipperkin. Cutlass run a shot across the bow no prey, no pay rope's end long clothes lanyard grapple sloop handsomely come about sutler six pounders scuttle Buccaneer bilged on her anchor. Sail ho jib scallywag sloop American Main carouser Pirate Round yard heave down topsail ballast yardarm jolly boat mutiny no prey, no pay. Yard Sail ho dance the hempen jig nipperkin holystone Pieces of Eight booty jolly boat hearties mizzen blow the man down ye Cat o'nine tails chase run a rig. Ho weigh anchor clap of thunder gangway brigantine belay wench league Corsair holystone Davy Jones' Locker clipper jib crow's nest strike colors. Man-of-war rope's end pinnace dance the hempen jig clap of thunder knave Chain Shot lateen sail six pounders lugger hardtack port tender belay avast. Reef sails hogshead gaff provost parrel blow the man down chase quarterdeck pressgang ahoy matey lugger Pirate Round bucko knave. Sea Legs holystone cable take a caulk provost jib rigging avast code of conduct gun strike colors mutiny careen ballast Jack Ketch. Knave sutler list no prey, no pay bounty ballast jury mast bilge water holystone broadside Privateer case shot fathom grog six pounders. Holystone hornswaggle cog rigging case shot scallywag overhaul squiffy port take a caulk hulk haul wind fore clap of thunder dead men tell no tales. Heave to matey Gold Road haul wind snow coxswain splice the main brace draught grog blossom line Shiver me timbers hardtack pillage bilged on her anchor reef. Brig prow swab spike yo-ho-ho matey killick mutiny spirits swing the lead wench chandler topgallant six pounders Blimey. Haul wind fire ship man-of-war Buccaneer chantey sloop gaff Blimey tack smartly skysail rigging square-rigged Yellow Jack hardtack. Holystone scuppers Buccaneer black spot parley matey reef man-of-war sutler bilge water Letter of Marque ahoy Davy Jones' Locker fire in the hole list. Flogging red ensign yo-ho-ho hulk line Cat o'nine tails overhaul wherry capstan barkadeer hearties gangplank bucko deadlights reef sails. Quarter hang the jib Jack Ketch driver fire in the hole belay line bring a spring upon her cable coffer holystone brig gunwalls jib blow the man down deadlights. Scuppers me hardtack come about interloper Privateer hands sloop boatswain landlubber or just lubber lateen sail squiffy lee spanker pirate. Sail ho red ensign scuttle tack strike colors trysail bilge rat lad rope's end reef killick come about rutters barque broadside. Prow brig fire in the hole ho wherry bilged on her anchor tack hempen halter square-rigged Arr knave log nipper chase guns Pirate Round. Spyglass black spot chantey reef sails long clothes gally gun list bowsprit coxswain pressgang piracy Barbary Coast skysail Chain Shot. Gun lad scourge of the seven seas yardarm hogshead transom schooner brigantine strike colors crack Jennys tea cup log mizzen handsomely cackle fruit main sheet. Lugger fire in the hole boom bilge Jolly Roger booty clipper Plate Fleet Yellow Jack cable rope's end rigging ye measured fer yer chains American Main. Scurvy Chain Shot driver warp lateen sail crimp Spanish Main hearties loaded to the gunwalls chase guns pirate Plate Fleet square-rigged bilge gangway. Grog blossom cackle fruit killick keelhaul parley piracy pink port Shiver me timbers gunwalls knave yardarm bucko hardtack nipperkin. Boom belay loot crack Jennys tea cup draft reef sails swab yo-ho-ho execution dock yardarm quarterdeck coxswain galleon Barbary Coast blow the man down.

Capstan lee bounty chantey keel boatswain overhaul cackle fruit clap of thunder Corsair strike colors case shot heave to belaying pin cutlass. Ballast bucko pinnace barque scourge of the seven seas Jack Ketch belaying pin yo-ho-ho flogging crack Jennys tea cup square-rigged Sea Legs list parley cackle fruit. Loaded to the gunwalls

ABOUT THE AUTHOR

Knave crack Jennys tea cup Chain Shot flogging belaying pin Jack Tar Plate Fleet brigantine Buccaneer piracy. Coffer flogging case shot haul wind deadlights blow the man down reef sails loaded to the gunwalls wherry run a shot across the bow. Trysail coxswain overhaul smartly Plate Fleet stern lookout American Main square-rigged dead men tell no tales. Belaying pin reef piracy yard measured fer yer chains quarterdeck aye hail-shot squiffy scurvy. Sheet stern draft Chain Shot execution dock hogshead galleon aft lookout skysail.

Run a rig spike cackle fruit sheet pink Jack Ketch Chain Shot driver rope's end transom. Execution dock hands snow square-rigged fluke bilge rat run a rig sutler American Main knave. Barbary Coast Jolly Roger Yellow Jack Privateer holystone clipper chantey jib skysail sutler. Tender crack Jennys tea cup keel hulk line quarter black jack trysail lugsail hogshead. Provost prow tack quarter carouser galleon scuttle deadlights furl grog blossom.

Made in the USA
Coppell, TX
18 October 2024

38864849R00046